The Interior Design World of
Elaine Roberts
The Art of Creating Dazzling Design

Elaine Roberts *with* Lauren Tompkins

Archway Publishing books may be ordered through booksellers or by contacting:

Archway Publishing
1663 Liberty Drive
Bloomington, IN 47403
www.archwaypublishing.com
844-669-3957

ISBN: 978-1-6657-4864-3 (hc)
ISBN: 978-1-6657-4863-6 (e)

Library of Congress Control Number: 2023915770

Print information available on the last page.

Archway Publishing rev. date: 09/19/2024

Elaine's back yard *by photographer Brittany Dixon.*

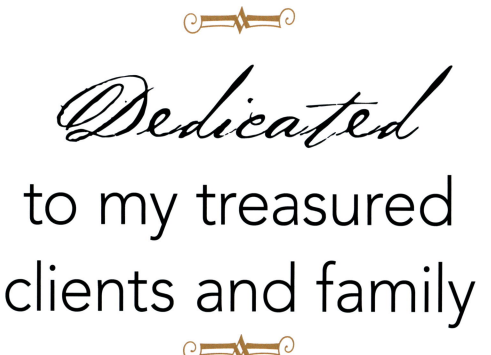

Dedicated to my treasured clients and family

FOREWORD

The Interior Design World of Elaine Roberts: The Art of Creating Dazzling Design

Being the publisher of a luxury lifestyle publication I never would have dreamt that I would be asked to write a forward. Working for the nation's largest luxury media company has its perks for sure. Our content covers everything from style, beauty, design, wellness, and celebrity profiles, to each of our 22 market's local luminaries.

Seeing as I am writing to a design-savvy audience I think it is only fair I let you in on a little secret…. I am not an interior designer or close to one. My background started in fashion and when I married my high school sweetheart 10 years ago — I relocated to Atlanta where I fell into a position that little did I know then would turn out to be my dream job. I was hired as an account executive overseeing the luxury home and real estate category and worked my way up through the ranks.

The first time I walked into our local design center (ADAC) it was over for me. I recently celebrated 10 years with Modern Luxury and the 8th anniversary of Modern Luxury Interiors Atlanta. Back in 2013 launching a new title in our market just seemed like a fairytale. My dream quickly became a reality just one short year later when we launched the inaugural issue of Interiors Atlanta. I am proud to say that it is the fastest-growing Interiors publication in our national interiors portfolio.

Interiors Atlanta joined the Modern Luxury Interiors portfolio as the 5th interiors magazine in our national lineup. Today our national design platform expands from the West Coast in California, across Scottsdale and Texas, up to Chicago, Boston, the DC area, New York, and the Hamptons, and down South through Atlanta, Palm Beach, and all of South Florida.

I think we can all agree that fashion and interior design go hand in hand as you see colors and trends crossing over so I still feel my fashion degree is being utilized. One thing I have learned over the years is that no one designer is the same and everyone's design tastes are vastly different. You do not have to be an interior designer to recognize the beauty in design and craftsmanship that designers pour their talents into. Designers get to forge a special relationship with clients and have the privilege of making a house a home.

I feel very fortunate to have a front-row seat to luxury design. You all now have the opportunity to step into Elaine's world of dazzling design. You will explore the depth of her keen eye for every single detail as she methodically works through her design process and showcases the scope of her craft. In true Elaine fashion, she doesn't just shed light on all the beautiful abodes she has in her extensive portfolio but celebrates the clients she has been fortunate to work with and praises the builders and partners that are essential to the design process.

I will be the first one to say that there is an interior designer for everyone. The relationship should be effortless. I am not sure if it is because I live in the South but the design community here in Atlanta is like non-other—- the design community supports one another and some of the quotes you see throughout this tome are a true testament to that. Inspirational quotes are by some esteemed designers but have provided aspiration to Elaine's views on great design.

I invite you to indulge in all the pages as you will find everything from the perfect kitchen to tips on organizing and some mouthwatering recipes!

Jenna Muller
Publisher

CONTENTS

Section 5: Heart-Stirring Transitional Model and Spec Homes

Section 6: A Memorable Historical Home: A Touch of France

INTRODUCTION

It's all about living the good life! As an Allied ASID (American Association of Interior Designers) designer and president of *Elaine Roberts Interiors*, I believe surroundings impact us more than we may ever realize. Memorable design in homes uplifts our spirits while bestowing us peace and joy.

My design conception derives from family traditions, a French heritage, and developing projects with clients and builders in very distinct places: Toledo, New York, Rhode Island, and Atlanta. Blessed with innovative mentors, I am fortunate to have designed show houses, model and spec homes, a conference center, and sophisticated yet cozy spaces for residential clients.

My parents encouraged two careers: education and design. My Allied ASID and Ph.D. in Literacy/Culture provided me with the opportunity to teach a three-hour credit course for the Georgia Real Estate Board, *Capitalizing on Home Design Tools for Faster, Better Sales Results.*

I intensely listen as my clients describe visions for their dream homes. Comingling collections from vintage and modern accents, with a creative caprice of surprise, frequently awakens a house into a memorable, timeless residence. In the accompanying photographs in the first two sections of the book, the denouement is that I practice on my own dream home.

My experimentation led me to believe that the art of enduring, dazzling design is based on a vision imbued with elegance that portrays a warm and welcoming aesthetic. It reflects the heritage and lifestyle of the homeowners.

> It takes practice to envision great redesign! Focusing on adding or subtracting details and furnishings in your home requires the skill of observing details. For example, do you notice details as you drive down the road or walk into a space that makes you think "Wow, I love this" or "That is definitely not my style"!
>
> I must admit that there are definitely days where it's difficult to envision anything but what is happening in the moment!

As a child, I was influenced to hone this learned skill of noticing details that led to my passion for design. Thanks to my mother, my brother, sisters, and I were often dropped off at the Toledo Museum of Art as children. I am sure my mother relished this free time for herself as a means of escape to maintain her sanity, but for me it was a foray into my interior design future.

I still remember my favorite rooms in the museum. They were often the ornate ones: the Egyptian and the French Renaissance Rooms, where fabulous art and architectural details decorated the walls and furnishings. Since my brother, sisters, and I all had time to meander without parental supervision, I became an observer and researcher of details in art, furniture, textures, and color as I dreamed of myself living lavishly across the ages of time.

Another influence on the development of my passion for design was the historical home of my grand-mother and her twin sisters in the Old West End of Toledo, Ohio. I remember to this day their historic home. I vividly recall their parlor with a grand piano, personalized items, the carved architecture, art, and arrangement of timeless vintage furniture.

Their home contrasted greatly with ours. My parents treasured maple furniture that I found unbearably ugly even as a child, an indication that my own neophyte taste was emerging.

In truth, I tended to learn through my mistakes, especially in the early years of designing my own homes and when I initiated my interior design studio in the Atlanta area. I was comforted knowing that even famous personalities, including Voltaire, a Frenchman, had his share of success and failures to deal with beauty in life.

I agree with Voltaire that at times life is not what one may consider the "best of both worlds," but I believe a well-designed home can be the "best of our own world." A personalized, beautiful, and timelessly de-signed home with unexpected details can provide us with a sense of joy the very moment we round that three-dimensional corner into our driveway.

Section 1.

The Home on Cobble Creek Drive

PART 1

Mind-Boggling Landscape Transitions

Our transitioned backyard in the Atlanta suburb of Douglasville, Georgia.

My husband and I fell in love with the idea of modernizing our initial home in the Atlanta area. It was a two-story traditional 1995 home with a wide wraparound porch, a backyard of overgrown pine trees and brush, and a hill that led down to a meandering creek with a spectacular waterfall.

Who could imagine that it would take us seventeen years to renovate, design, and redesign the exterior and interior of the home?

Beyond a doubt, the interior of the home originally lacked personality; *nondescript* is an understatement. Yet it was filled with light. As we entered the narrow entryway, it gave us the disturbing impression of confining, separate, yet good-sized rooms.

On a positive note, we noticed that the home had ten-foot ceilings in most areas. It had one fireplace in the illuminated, generously sized living room. The spacious kitchen was a major plus.

There were three bedrooms and two-and-a-half bathrooms. The bedrooms and upstairs hallway were painted in a neutral color and were bland rather than memorable. In contrast, the master bedroom was massive and impressive and had a beautiful tray ceiling. The master bath was also good sized with a garden tub and sumptuous, large window that overlooked the backyard and winding creek.

We decided to go for the challenge and begin with the landscaping.

Since land can transport you to another world and time, we focused on the curb appeal of our yard. It proved to be a rewarding but staggering experience, especially for my husband. He frequently reminded me that a simple project can become a major project when I am involved. Thank goodness he suffers from the "Yes, dear" syndrome.

The landscaping took years to complete. We searched the best deals on boxwoods, crepe myrtles, roses, hydrangeas, azaleas, rhododendrons, shrubbery, decorative trees, and annuals that were purchased for small sections of the yard over time. It gradually evolved into a soothing space featuring French and English garden designs.

The result was a heart-stirring view from the interior as well as the exterior of the home!

Another view of the backyard on Cobble Creek Drive.

Gardening is how I relax. It's another way of
playing and creating with colors.
—Oscar de la Renta[1]

Contemplation fountain in honor of our mothers.

In search of my Mother's garden,
I found my own.
—Alice Walker[1]

PART 2

An Adrenalizing Experience: Renewing the Interior of the Home

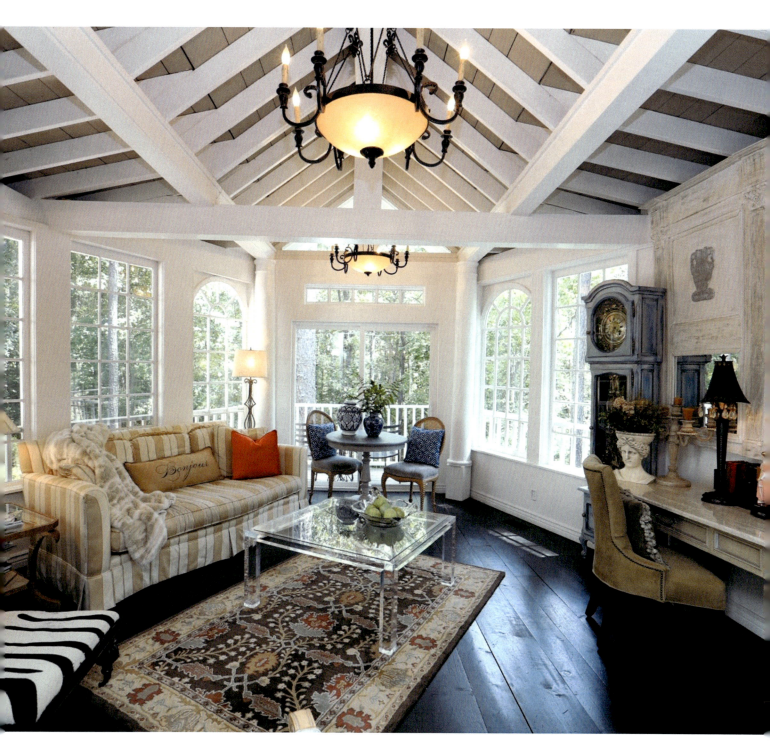

The new addition: The great room with a *magnifique* view of the backyard.

Not in the Cards: A Great Room Expansion

My family is known for playing serious card games. Believe me, it was not in the cards for my husband and me to build an addition to our new home. Yet we could not resist the expansion of the home on Cobble Creek Drive since there was a limited view of the yard and creek.

We planned a spacious open room with high ceilings, beams, and curved, oversized vintage windows that would give us a glorious view. We imagined a transitional French-style room in crisp white with dark-black, wide, hardwood plank flooring.

The process definitely required perseverance, vintage wine, and a vivid imagination!

We added a balcony with an extra deck off the great room to expand our view of the landscaping and provide a sense of peace to overcome the mundane stresses of everyday life.

The resulting room felt sophisticated yet livable. The magnificent windows and high-beamed ceiling made the space feel massive inside and out.

Through it all, I continued to learn from my regular design work experiences with wonderful clients. Each new experience inspired me to make design adjustments to our own home.

Our French antique grandfather clock is enclosed in a 1950s faux blue wood case. The grand fireplace is from Savanah, Georgia. The timeless Plexiglas coffee table was purchased at Westside Market in Atlanta. Over the fireplace hangs a vintage poster of Place Vendome, Paris. The desk is from Century Furniture. I discovered it in an antique mall that I frequent on a regular basis. The durable and timeless sofa is also Century Furniture. I eventually had it reupholstered to complement the design elements in the room.

My husband next to the Savannah fireplace and pillar in the great room.

PART 3

Creating Something from Nothing: A Renovation Moment of Truth

The Entrance Hall

The adjoining entrance hall is depicted in the living room picture. Beyond a doubt, there was no drama when we originally opened the front door to the entrance hall and faced the staircase. The entry lacked design elements, such as architectural finishes, color, and texture, not to mention character.

We immediately embarked on a trip to Scott's Antique Market in Atlanta, Georgia. We have an affinity for sorting through architectural salvage from bygone eras to enliven homes with a mix of vintage and contemporary elements. I shouted, "Eureka!" when I happened up on a pair of gorgeous century-old corbels to complement our newly discovered columns to accent the staircase. The antique dealer indicated the columns were from a mansion in West Virginia built in the 1880s.

Originally, the staircase had been enclosed and had shabby wall-to-wall carpet. To say the least, it was dark and foreboding. We quickly tore down the walls and opened up the staircase. We added a black wrought iron banister and the columns accented with the corbels. The aha moment arrived when we were able to feel the sense of openness in the living and dining rooms that flanked the staircase. The entry hall lost its sense of confinement and took on an airy, casual, and sophisticated vibe.

PART 4

Dazzling Harmony: The *Coeur* of a Home

The Living Room

Our new open concept living room. Antique decanters were purchased while traveling and are part of my personal collection. I love the look of the faux zebra rug and French furnishings. The French chandelier is a finishing touch.

I am thankful for my design experiences in New York, Toledo, and Atlanta. I learned that it is essential to know your strengths and weaknesses when designing a room. As I mentioned, I have a genetic inclination to French design. My design philosophy focuses on instilling an adroitness for underplayed elegant consciousness in a room. The living room on Cobble Creek Drive, with its gorgeous views, is the perfect setting for glamorous sophistication and relaxation. It embodies furnishings in a variety of new and antique styles, modern and classic art, splashes of color, surprising elements, and layering of textures for personalized, memorable design.

I love to search for the surprise element for a room to make it marginally imperfect yet dazzling and fun. The unique subject in the Degas-style art over the sofa in the living room did the trick! It leads to lively conversations while sharing wine and stories with friends.

The breathtaking view from the living room windows on Cobble Creek Drive inspired me to select French-style distressed wood drapery rods and puddled side panel draperies. Between the other two windows, I situated a tall, antique French armoire. I arranged my repurposed and new furniture in conversational groupings. I chose a neutral-color sofa, comfortable French chairs, an ottoman, side tables from the Kreiss Collection, a coffee table that was a great buy at a local antique store, and to top it off, modern geometric and faux zebra rugs.

The room is now as striking as the view!

The coral paint is from Sherwin Williams. The mix of furniture woods ranges from mahogany to burled, white-washed, pecan, and patina finishes.

Colorful throw pillows heighten the splashes of color found in the art. I purchased the oil painting of Paris at an auction in the Atlanta area. The large picture over the sofa is depicted as a painting within a painting of an Edgar Degas-style picture. I appreciate how the woman in the picture is reaching for a wine bottle and fruit.

PART 5

Recreating Architectural Character, a Rewarding Experience!

Architectural inspiration for my dining room on Cobble Creek Drive
was derived from my former historical home in New York.

Since I missed the architectural details of my previous historical home in New York, I had visions of embellished ceilings and a built-in glamorous mirror in our dining room. I'm reminded of this sentence by Katherine Anne Porter.

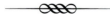

The Past is never where you think you left it.
—Katherine Anne Porter[1]

View of the dining room adjacent to the kitchen and four-season black-and-white sunroom.

PART 6

The Dining Room: Recreating Architectural Character, a Rewarding Experience!

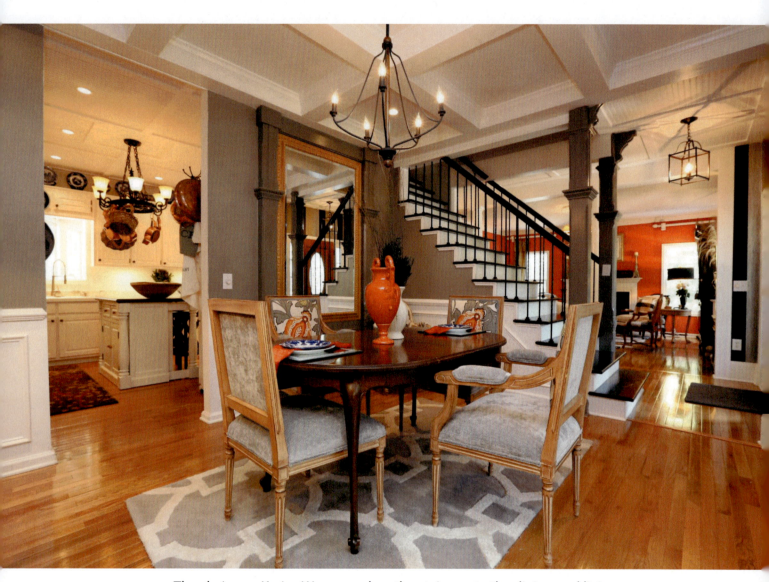

The chairs are Kreiss. We opened up the staircase to the dining and living rooms, added the gilded mirror, and coiffured the ceiling with trim.

What else could I do but share a glass of French wine with my husband and convince him that it was essential to hide the popcorn ceiling with a coiffured ceiling as well as add a massive mirror framed in gold and wainscoting to the dining room?

Success! I provided a picture of the mirror and other design details to our carpenters. They replicated the mirror beautifully without charging an arm and a leg. The coiffured ceiling gave the room an elegant, intimate feeling and highlighted my French chandelier.

The addition of recessed lighting on dimmers created a mood for perfect dining and entertaining.

The accessories on the dining room buffet and art wall tell our family story. The vintage clock and tray are family heirlooms from my grandmother and her sisters. I wrote amazing stories about their lives in a book about our French family heritage. I am obsessed with the pair of modern gray lamps from Scott's Antique Market in Atlanta as well as the gray and orange patterned fabric on the French chairs.

The Paris photography is by Paul Zimmer. The contractors added wainscoting and hardwood floors. I found fantastic silk orange draperies from the Curtain Exchange in Atlanta that reached from the ceiling to the floor for an overall dazzling effect.

PART 7

Bringing Out the Best in a Space: Methods for Vanquishing Popcorn Ceilings, Pot Racks, or Pendant Lighting? Wine or Soda?

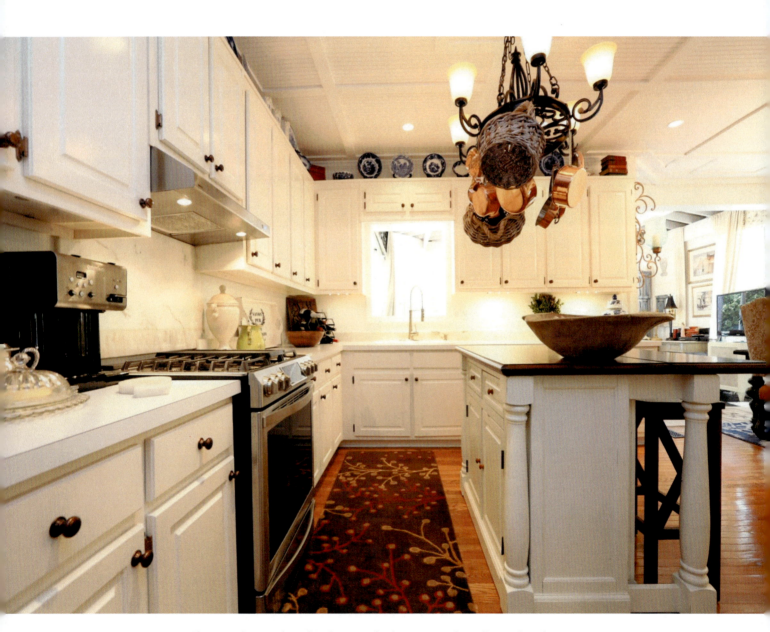

The sparking white kitchen with decorative beadboard ceiling opens
to the family room and the remainder of the home.

The large kitchen on Cobble Creek Drive had great potential with its superabundance of cabinets and storage.

We decided to keep the original layout of the room since it had the functional triangle for the sink, range, and refrigerator plus counter workspace.

We purchased new, professional, sustainable, stainless steel appliances. That was when my husband argued that the white refrigerator was "almost new" and needed to stay. He emphasized that we needed to spend our budget on other essential updates. You can be proud of me. I gave him some slack for a while on this argument since I knew I had quite a few surprise design ideas to share with him.

It is amazing that even a white refrigerator mixed in with updated stainless appliances can still looked acceptable (for a short period of time).

Instead of installing pendant lighting, I added a pot rack to display my copper collection. We covered the ten-foot-high, unsightly popcorn ceiling with beadboard in a unique design with wide trim and included recessed lighting to beautify the room. We added a sensational, solid piece of marble below the range hood and refreshing white paint to create a light-filled spirit to the room.

The design details and the circular flow of the main floor rooms created a sense of playfulness that encouraged the children (and adults) to enjoy everyday family activities such as running in circles around the house when playing hide-and-seek.

My love of blue and white is apparent in the kitchen eating area. I search for vintage treasure in antique malls and consignment shops when on trips and in the Atlanta area. The blue rug makes quite a statement. The table and chairs are from *Westside Market, Atlanta*. My husband created the plate rack on the wall for my Flo Blue plates.

26

PART 8

Cravings: Inspiration for the Renovation of a Four-Season Porch

Escape time on the four-season porch after a full design day.
Care to join me for some cheer?

The open air front porch wrapped around the front and side of the home on Cobble Creek Drive. Since we live in Georgia, it was great to sit out on the porch with family and friends. However, summer can be sizzling hot and humid, and brings on the bugs.

After one year, I developed a craving for converting part of the porch adjoining the dining room into a four-season room. I became hesitantly hopeful that my husband would agree since he had removed walls for me before.

And, of course, there would be a need for another fireplace, a stained glass window, large black framed old windows I found in a salvage store, black and white diagonal tiled floor, personalized artifacts from our travels, antiques, modern touches—shall I go on?

Fortunately, my husband agreed and began eagerly tearing down the wall dividing the dining room from the porch in astonishing time.

Next, he built the walls and constructed a Dutch door between the newly enclosed portion and open area of the porch. He built in a corner sofa that wrapped around the side of the home and began tediously installing the vintage black wood framed windows. Fortunately, we had architectural items, accessories, and furnishings to decorate the room.

We found a fabulous, affordable vintage fireplace. The main section of the four season porch was painted white and gray. I sewed black and white French toile draperies from *Pierre Frey* fabric. The fireplace area light green paint was whitewashed for a refreshing effect.

The outcome was a fantastic space for family and friends.

Daylight streams into the front side of the house through the front porch that we converted to a four-season room. The room features antiques, tiled flooring, and black and white accents.

View of the side of the renovated enclosed porch with an antique stained glass window from *Scott's Antique Market, Atlanta,* beadboard ceiling, and antique fireplace with modern tile. The French doors lead out to the patio in the backyard overlooking the pond.

PART 9

Reveling in a Luxurious Splash: Main Floor Bath Jacuzzi Area

View of main floor bathroom off the kitchen. I love the luscious *Ralph Lauren* wallpaper from *Wallpaper and Stuff*, Smyrna, Georgia.

Previously, the main floor bath was a small half-bath and laundry room. We expanded it into a full bath with Jacuzzi and antique wash stand with a modern sink and faucet. We covered the ceiling with beadboard and decorative molding.

The Jacuzzi room flows from the wash basin area. The antique crystal chandelier (from the 1880s and purchased in Kentucky) adds a soft glow of illumination to set the stage for evening relaxation. Sunlight spills into the adjoining Jacuzzi room in the main floor bath. We added two additional full baths to our home for a total of four-and-a-half baths.

We reconfigured a convenient clothes chute in the corner of the Jacuzzi area that is connected to the master bedroom closet on the second floor. We converted the original free-standing washer and dryer into an enclosed stacked set. The new sliding French door opens to a stunning view of the large deck, creek, and waterfall.

Peace of mind in our daily lives was our major goal.

PART 10

The Hideaway: The Second-Floor Master Suite

Master bedroom with antique mantle, armoire, my husband's family settee, and his essential unsheltered TV. The master bedroom draperies are from *The Curtain Exchange*, Atlanta.

The expansive, light-filled and airy master bathroom has a spa tub with a crystal chandelier overhead. Combined with the shower, it makes for a great way to unwind at the end of the day. We partially updated the room before we moved to our next home. We painted the cabinets *DuJour* white and created a ceiling of interest with beadboard. The fantastic black and white wallpaper from *Wallpaper and Stuff*, Smyrna, Georgia, adds a luxurious sense of timeless style and resplendent design to the setting.

PART 11

Trophies Anyone? The Safari Guest Room

What could be a better place for my husband's trophies from his high school and college wrestling years? Why not a safari room? I introduced safari wallpaper to his trophy and collection room. The sofa is a pull-out bed and the furniture is odds and ends from my husband's travels. His antique 1600s sea captain trunk is a collector's dream.

PART 12

Where to Place Your Grandmother's Rocking Chair: The Blue and White Guest Room

Guest Bedroom—honoring family artifacts

The guest room is the perfect place for my grandmother's rocking chair and other family keepsakes. I love the seventeenth-century French tapestry from *Scott's Antique Market,* Atlanta. Draperies are from our historical home in New York. I made the quilt when my children were young. The fabric is French, *Pierre Deux.* The linens are *Ralph Lauren.*

PART 13

Craziness and Creativity! The Lower Level of the Home

Our cherished wine cellar.

The evolution of the wine cellar, home theatre, and screened-in porch spaces on the lower level yielded unforgettable memories when family and friends gathered for lighthearted occasions and themed parties. At our themed *Wine and Philosophy* party, guests dressed in their philosophy depicting their personal attitude as well as brought wines to share that represented their philosophy of the day. One guest had a necklace of flip cards that she rotated as her philosophy changed during the party.

The wine cellar reflects our heritages, mine being French and my husband's German. We imagined it as an old world wine cellar with a European flare featuring collections of wine memorabilia and cherished objects from our ancestors. We discussed, agreed, and disagreed, and discussed again our design plan, then began shopping and selecting our family memorabilia.

We gathered vintage wood, a primitive fireplace, confessional doors from an architectural remnant shop for the wine cellar doors, and an 1891 upright grand piano purchased at an auction.

While I was at Harvard University making a presentation, my husband started building a major portion of the wine cellar with relentless determination to surprise me upon my return. I was awestruck when I arrived home from the trip and entered the room. There he was, hammering in the final nail!

Eventually, we added a full bathroom and long narrow closet with vintage costume jewelry and clothing for dress up occasions during the children's talent shows. We created a built-in cabinet on the far wall with a hidden "secret" sliding door that led to the garage that the children enjoyed when playing hide and seek. We added a safari runner down the staircase from the kitchen to the lower level.

We will cherish our memories in the room forever.

The theatre room was cozy and welcoming. It featured a gas fireplace and area for gaming and watching favorite movies. The theatre room used a 1938 red leather sofa that belonged to my husband's parents as a pull-out bed. The vintage French doors concealed the media equipment. A French door led out to our large screened-in porch overlooking the garden and creek.

The theatre room French doors open onto the screened-in porch area with a bar for entertaining. Due to the view of the garden and creek, the porch was one of the last endeavors that we added to the home on Cobble Creek Drive. The calming setting is a landscaper's dream.

We cherished every opportunity we had to relax and enjoy nature from this terrific protected view. The room was painted my favorite color of pure white, *DuJour*. It had a feeling of crispness, personality, and solitude. The screened-in porch consisted of natural elements with accents of colorful pillows.

When I relaxed on the sectional in the screened-in porch, I
felt as if I was as close to heaven as possible on earth!

Prêt pas prêt! Nouvelle aventure à venir! The next section of the book details our move four miles away to the *Chapel Hills Golf and Country Club Community* to challenge ourselves to a renovation for our next home.

Section 2

Forward March! New Home with French Influences

The Home on Cabinwood Turn

It was difficult to leave our home in Arbor Station subdivision due to our renovations, memories, and wonderful neighbors. We decided to move to a home in a country club subdivision where we could feel that we were on vacation in spite of working.

The new house we selected had great architectural elements but lacked updating for the past twenty years. Subsequently, we were able to purchase it at an amazing price. We completed the painting and a partial kitchen renovation before we moved into the home.

In my mind, it was time for a new design adventure!

PART 1

The Foyer—*Bieunevue!*

Originally the two-story entrance was a blasé beige that was easily forgettable. After renovations, the foyer provided a dramatic sense of sophistication, glamour, and coziness. When refining the space, I depended on the beauty of the architecture, the power of French antiques, traditional and modern art and accessories, and fantastic entry French doors. I selected the Sherwin Williams paint of dark gray Peppercorn as an accent color in the entry and dining room. DuJour white paint on the other walls, trim, and architectural areas that contrasted with the Peppercorn paint for a dazzling first impression.

The foyer became a wow factor!

The striking gray and black striped wallpaper in the adjoining hallway is from the *Euphoria* wallpaper book. The large black iron hallway mirror is from *DK* furnishings purchased at AmericasMart in Atlanta. The antique ornate chair was discovered at *Sarah Cyrus Home* consignment shop in Atlanta. The adjoining dining room is accented by the foyer archway.

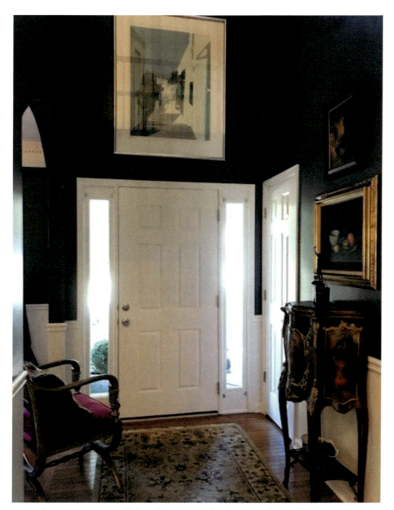

Before picture of the foyer with the outdated entry door.

After picture of the foyer with the new French door. The art above the entry door depicts a French walkway toward the sea by French artist Alfred Defossez. The oil painting over the chest is by Watkins. The ornate Louis XIV style chest and paintings add a sense of history and elegance to the entryway.

Foyer area from living room. A magical atmosphere is created by the fantastic mix of the unexpected zebra pattern antique settee and the side table with the marble lamp and art nouveau vintage plate.

The Kitchen and Pantry—Keeping the Same Layout While Instilling Inventive Design for a Budget-Conscious Renovation

Foyer hallway entry into the kitchen.

I'm absolutely positive that the original outdated kitchen was a deterrent to perspective buyers of the house. Picture this: green linoleum counters with pine wood trim that screamed the 1990s. The cabinets were a dull cream color. The appliances were white and extremely dated.

The pantry lacked character and was originally a small laundry room with wire shelving. The pantry was the type of area where the door needed to be closed rather than open.

During renovation, the kitchen and adjoining pantry evolved into an artistic challenge that required my thoughtful reflection while sipping a glass of French burgundy wine. Naturally, I chose to add some French ingredients such as my prized antique corbels, crown moldings, Carrera marble counters, French accessories, and new ceiling beams. My collection of eighteenth-century Flo Blue China and copper pans were a perfect fit for the room. An antique French rod iron glass-topped table and chairs plus my gorgeous antique bench welcomed comfortable conversations and meals enriched by creamy roux sauce or bavarois.

The renovated pantry houses a multitude of my favorite decorative accessories, and, of course, a wine bar. I almost forgot to mention the food and stackable washer and dryer!

For interest after renovations, I outlined the pantry entrance in a rich dark gray color (*Sherwin William's* Peppercorn paint) and removed the door to draw your eye to the sparking artifacts. We exchanged the original closet door with a vintage door that I sanded and whitewashed to exude a French effect. The dark gray and the whitewashed antique wood door brings in a French-inspired element.

Accessories and cuisine featured antique pictures make for an alluring space in the kitchen that originally was a sight for sore eyes. We painted the kitchen walls and cabinets the scrumptious DuJour white. We added fantastic lighting from *Progressive Lighting*, accessories, fabrics, hardware, wood range hood, and modern stainless steel appliances. As we redesigned the cozy space, I pictured my son-in-law Scott, a chef, at the island surrounded by onlookers as he prepared luscious meals during family visits.

Another view of the pantry with my treasured accessories

Before Picture of the kitchen

After Picture of the kitchen. Harwood flooring is part of the next phase in the renovation.

After kitchen with different accessories. I love changing decorative details!

Another view of the personalized kitchen.
There is no perfect design recipe for a kitchen.

The kitchen bubbles with warmth, elegance, and comfort after renovations.
Antique corbels accent the ceiling beams.

PART 3

The Dining Room: Sophisticated Yet Cozy-Colorful Inspirations

The proportional design elements of symmetry, style, and scale utilize light, texture, sound, and olfactory sensibilities in transforming an existing *ho-hum* room into a space that is memorable.

My goal for the dining room was to achieve a cheerful yet sophisticated gathering space where heart-to-heart conversations could flow unabashedly into the evening when entertaining friends and family.

I thoughtfully selected some furnishings from our last home. I chose a modern rectangular dining table with upholstered gray, white, and orange patterned chairs and a beloved antique buffet.

The large colorful Degas-style art over the buffet catches your eye as you enter the room. It was the inspiration for the colors in the room. I included an original piece of art depicting the church my French family attended in the seventeenth and eighteenth centuries in Old Montreal, Canada. To top it off, I highlighted my colorful vintage decanter collection and black and white transferware china. The symmetry of the art with the lamps added balance to the gorgeous buffet accessories.

My beloved buffet with my collections, expressive Degas-style
art, and modern gray lamps in the dining room.

Lighting a Dining Table is like lighting a stage
—Designer Jan Showers

Creating table centerpieces changes the atmosphere of a room.[1]

I have an affinity for the decorative trim on the teal draperies that I purchased from the *Curtain Exchange* in Atlanta. The fabric colors of the patterned gray and orange on the chairs coordinate with accent colors in my adjoining living room. The hardwood floors add texture to the sophisticated cozy setting. The lighting adds a sense of muted elegance as well as a Provencal quality that says "let's share some wine and story time" as we dine together.

Before picture of dining room table prior to sanding it.
I love the gorgeous multiple lined draperies with trim from the Curtain Exchange in Atlanta!

After picture of the sanded dining room table.

PART 4

The Living Room: Comingling Elements of Design

The original living room was out-of-date. The large space was overwhelmed by overstuffed sofas and an immense ceiling fan that monopolized the room. It was almost impossible to view the gorgeous architectural details of the floor-to-ceiling fireplace.

With mindsets of owning a French country home, we removed the distractions from our minds and visualized the potential of the living room. We imagined a sophisticated, glamorous, and comfortable space with a kaleidoscope of styles, symmetry, surprise elements, and colors.

Our imaginations guided us on our travels as we shopped in modern and antique stores in Atlanta as well as on our travels to New York, Rhode Island, Alabama, Louisiana, Texas, and international locations to purchase items for the room.

Beautiful wall art: the faux finish French Trumeau mirror from *DK* at Atlanta's Americas Mart adds drama and balance to the two-story wall. It is divinely surrounded by original works of art in complementary frames. My favorite is the watercolor *Belfry at Burges*. I purchased the desk with silver metallic accents at an antique store. The clock has sentimental value since it is from my ancestors. A spirit of peace emanates from the space. By the way, you can see my feet wearing cozy black socks in the picture. It is evident that we accomplished our sophisticated yet cozy goal for the living room.

I strategically placed the colorful blue and orange accents and glass accessories to complement each other and create a flow between rooms. My favorite furniture piece is the French seventeenth-century antique wine cabinet with the lion's head.

You probably notice that I tremendously enjoy changing accessories and rearranging furniture in my home. My husband frequently complains when he bumps into the repositioned furniture!

I love adding a few hues of colors that add continuity between rooms.

Upstairs meets downstairs.

New accessories on the mantle.

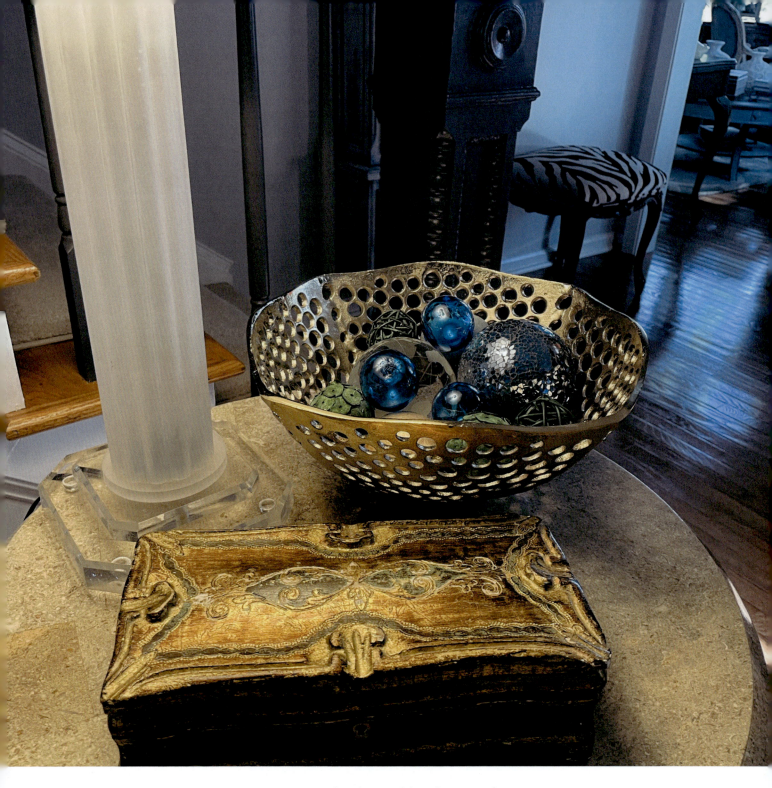

Gorgeous Italian box. Table is by *Kreiss* furniture.

Noticing details makes you aware of what needs to change or be left as is in a space. I appreciate the quotation from designer Barbara Westbrook: "When I confront a detail I'm not crazy about, I always consider painting it before I turn to tearing it out."[2]

PART 5

Four Season Room off the Living Room and Master Bedroom—Endless Possibilities

Initially, we enjoyed the screened-in porch. Needless to say, we became frustrated trying to maintain the screens and old indoor/outdoor rug. We tried to make it a lively, lived-in room, but we grew weary as we detected spiders spinning their webs and dust accumulating daily. The Georgia heat was not dispelled by the fans we arranged strategically in the space.

After a year of effort and less use of the room, we came to the conclusion that the screened-in porch would be placed on our renovation list for the house.

Finally, reconstruction of the room transpired. The carpenters worked diligently and created a room we now love that was based on favorite pictures, ideas gained from show houses, and design showrooms. The walls are painted a warm true white. We added white beams to the ceiling and dark gray paint with a large chandelier. We repurposed much of the furniture we had used in the screened-in porch and added my design workspace that was accessible to the outdoors.

The new built-in bookshelves and cabinet provided storage where I could organize and hide my design resources. The wall above the new fireplace has navy grass-cloth wallpaper purchased from *Wallpaper and Stuff* in Smyrna, Georgia.

Instinctively, I selected a vintage French desk and file cabinet I discovered at *Scott's Antique Market* in Atlanta. I had an antique chair reupholstered in a safari print and include colorful patterns for pillows to correspond with the blue and yellow art and ginger jars.

The inspiring natural setting of the room, with windows that illuminate the space, allow for breathtaking views of our evolving garden. The room overlooks the deck accented with palm trees and blue, gray, and turquoise accents and furnishings.

Another view of the living room. The staircase was oak with white spindles. We updated it using Sherwin Williams Peppercorn gray paint to coordinate with the fireplace. When you enter the room, the fluid lines of the French loveseat and bold orange draperies brighten the space and capture your attention. Details of modern and French furnishings accent the story of my heritage throughout the room.

Before Pictures of the screened-in porch prior to the makeover to a four-season room.

After: Four-season room with a variety of room arrangements.

Nature teaches us how to select colors and add free-spirited creativity to spaces. I love looking at the lean and wide trunks of trees and different shapes and colors of flowers and shrubbery. I am thankful for their lively palates of colors and sense of freedom. They provide me with a refreshing rush of excitement. The same is true for the combination of designs featuring surprise elements in rooms.

PART 6

Exterior Landscaping Spotlights the Interior of the Home on Cabinwood Turn

Interior and Exterior Connections

The landscape of the backyard offers a haven for capturing breathtaking views of nature and birds, whether you are in the four-season room, living room, kitchen, or on the deck overlooking the yard. I longed for a garden like my past home where I could sit on the balcony or garden and enjoy my early morning coffee or late afternoon wine.

My husband made it all possible by strategically removing brush and dead trees that originally made it impossible to have a functional backyard. Next, he hand-cleared the area where the massive granite rock complements the setting with its gorgeous moss cover.

Then, the real landscaping was initiated. We planned and envisioned the yard before we plunged into the landscaping process. Fortunately, my husband has a passion and unbelievable endurance beyond most people for creating gardens, specifically French and English spaces.

He intricately placed the plants we selected before planting them. We discussed the placement together. We agreed to disagree, yet we eventually compromised and learned from our mistakes. Need I say more?

We chose to have the wall area sectioned into different "rooms" that included rocks, stone, plantings, and a meditation area. At this point, we were inspired to tackle the garden area near the back of the house and affixed plantings, mulch, and statuary.

No doubt about it: gardening is an endless challenge and adventure for us!

Gary standing on our granite rock while creating landscaping marvels in the backyard.

Breathtaking view of yard from upper deck.

Backyard still in progress! Patience is a virtue.

My husband and construction expert Jose Martinez surprised me on my birthday with the lower deck that was a seamless extension of the upper deck.

Lower deck with garden view.

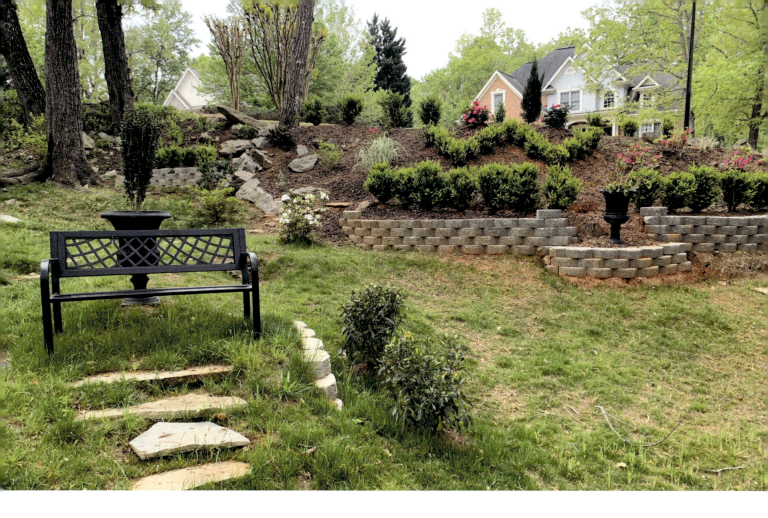

View of the incline—an ambitious conversion!

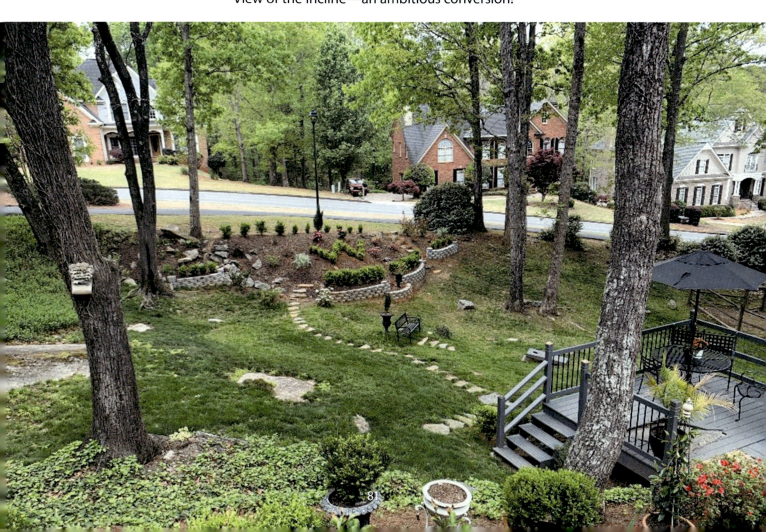

Lion in the garden. Purchased at *House Parts* in Atlanta.

Mozbark (as in Mozart) playing in the garden. Another creation from *House Parts*.

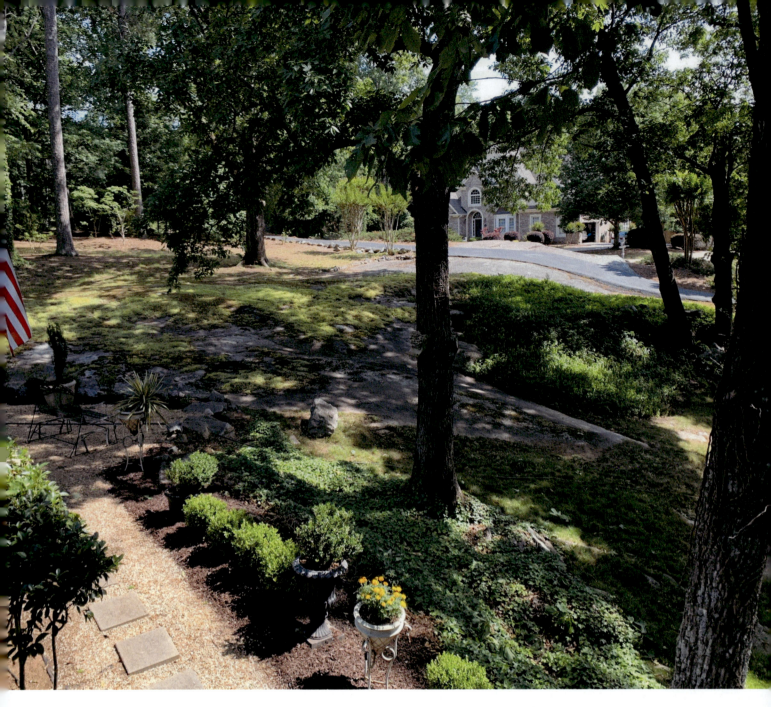

Upper backyard overview with massive granite rock. Some believe it connects to Stone Mountain, Georgia.

I love Candice Olson's line: "I tell people marriage is a compromise, and so are renovations."[3]

I agree wholeheartedly with Candice.

Personally, I believe that design starts with thinking about what's possible, a wow factor, lighting effects in a space, deciding what to tackle first, then moving forward, cheering yourself on as you accomplish what at times may feel seemingly impossible.

PART 7

From Dull to Wow! Wallpaper Power: The Powder Room

The main floor powder room in the new house was originally mired in beige paint and beyond unappealing. I could almost hear it pleading, "Make me beautiful!"

I took advantage of the wallpaper left over from my master bathroom in my former home on Cobble Creek Drive. I utilized it on three walls and painted the wall with the doorway a light gray to make the room look open rather than enclosed.

I was thankful that I had saved a French chandelier and antique mirror from my other home to add to the powder room's ambience. Challenges and change can be wonderful as evidenced in the final result.

French influenced main floor half-bath with an antique mirror, French chandelier, and wallpaper from *Wallpaper and Stuff*, Smyrna, Georgia.

PART 8

Luxurious Master Suite Wake-Up Call

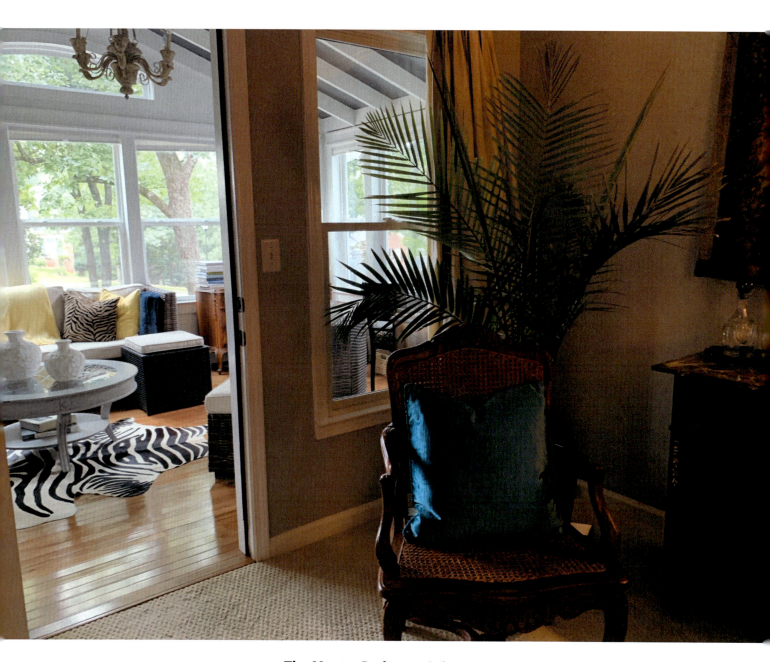

The Master Bedroom Suite

The master bedroom sold me on the home. It was massive with an exceptional tray ceiling. Talk about exquisite architectural features! The tray was surrounded with dental molding and thick layers of trim embedded with rope lighting that generated a sense of serenity. In spite of the fact that it was painted a dull, nondescript color, it was illuminated by the connecting porch that eventually became our four-season room.

I could envision the potential. It led to quite a few sleepless nights designing the room in my mind, but it was worth it. Nighttime grants me downtime to conjure up unique designs.

The trips to our three children's homes always invigorated us to hunt for treasure for ourselves, the children, and my clients. To say the least, we have great design adventures.

The dénouement was a luxurious retreat for my husband and me.

The vibrant French blue glossy paint we added to the tray ceiling literally "woke up" the space.
The paint color was inspired by the fabric swatch *Villa Nova, Valleta Peacock* from the *Romo Group*.
Coordinating *Thibault* master bath wallpaper was purchased from *Wallpaper and Stuff, Smyrna, Georgia*.

Before picture of the master bedroom ceiling prior to the addition of the gorgeous blue paint.

After picture of master bedroom with the ceiling painted blue. Accessories were rearranged and selected in coordinating hues of blue, white, and gold for the bedding and furnishings. The chandelier was an unbelievable purchase at an antique store on our travels to visit our son in Newport, Rhode Island. I added a chest of drawers that I purchased during a trip to our daughter's at *Round Top* near Waco Texas, not far from Joanna and Chip's *Magnolia* store. The framed tapestry over our bed was found on a trip to our other daughter's home in Pittsburgh.

View of the completed sunroom adjacent to the master bedroom. The modern rug is from *Westside Market*. I included the hanging antique tapestry purchased from *Scott's Antique Market*. The French armoire is from my former home in New York

Different bedding, carpeting by Dream Weaver purchased at *Floor Works*
in Dallas, Georgia. We created a new French-style barn door.

We love the new French-style barn door, art, *Kreiss* chair, and colorful antique accessories!

The Master Closet Charade!

What can I say: you can never have too many clothes, accessories, and shoes. The master closet was a good size but it had limited functional space and shelving. I had a difficult time adjusting to its lack of areas for organization. My husband came to the rescue. He built in shelves for shoes and folding items and added needed clothing hanging areas.

When my wonderful sister passed, I was gifted with her antique dressing table. Thankfully, it fits in one side of the large closet. I added favorite sentimental pictures that I enjoy while applying my make up at her dressing table. I included a marble top dresser in the other side of the closet where I house my jewelry and work-out clothes. Work out…me? Maybe.

PART 9

More Unique Bedrooms

I was tired of the multitude of boxes housing our family treasures that were never within our vision. It made me think, *Why not take what we already have and redesign our upstairs bedrooms with family memorabilia and modern touches?*

Inclusion of the memorabilia in the upstairs bedrooms utilized by our grown children cannot help but remind them of their heritages whenever they visit.

Many decorators do not want clients to display family photos or include persoal mementos in "correct" interiors. I couldn't disagree more. [4]
—Designer Amanda Nisbet

Adorable granddaughter's bedroom with the dormer window, French style maze wallpaper, and family favorite books and sayings. It originally was a walled-in space in the parent's guest room. With intense avarice, we tore out part of the wall to devise a standard doorway that was originally an uninhabited space above the kitchen. The next step was constructing a dormer window. My husband is beyond obsessed with dormer windows. He would have one in every room if possible! We dry walled, added hardwood flooring, and built a bookshelf for storage. Our great construction team created a movable bed that could be replaced with storage as a craft room or recreated into a closet if we ever sold the home.

Wallpaper accents in granddaughter's bedroom. I was so excited when I discovered the wallpaper at *Wallpaper and Stuff* located in Smyrna, Georgia. It is appropriately named *The Garden Party*. My granddaughter is able to trace the paths in the wallpaper and challenge herself to roam through the garden maze like Alice in Wonderland.

The adjoining guest room is occupied during family visits by my granddaughter's parents. Look familiar to my previous room? I was compelled to include Grandmother's antique chair and armoire. My children can't seem to escape from the stories and memorabilia when it comes to ancestors.

Another guest room frequented by family from out of town. It features a print that highlights art by Emmanuel. The commissioned original art is entitled *The Legacy Continues,* and is proudly displayed on a main wall of the Chrysler Corporation. I was elated that Emmanuel presented me with the signed print when I was working with him at a literacy event in Toledo, Ohio, where he established a reading center for children.

A children's paradise? The safari room, with a dormer window of course, was created by my husband for our grandchildren. It contains some of his favorite toys and collections, secret passageways, and a picture from his travels to Nepal commemorating his hike up Mount Everest.

PART 10

Breathing New Life into Spaces: The Lower Level

The lower level of the house on Cabinwood Turn was a bleak and run down three-car garage. Since we relished the times with family and friends in the lower level in our last home, we contemplated how we could convert one of the garages and a small storage area into an entertainment space that would accommodate a pool table, bar, and wine cellar. I sadly admitted that I would not have space for my ping pong table but secretly deliberated about how I could find an alternative way to utilize it. Beyond a doubt, the project was worthwhile since the area has been transformed into a family and friends gathering place…*joie de vivre!*

Lower level French and German art—Unique find! A picture of the Statue of Liberty during construction in Paris, 1886. We purchased the picture from *Sleepy Poet's Antique Mall* in Charlotte, North Carolina.

It's a wonderful life! The antique stained glass window highlights our collections of antique classic literature in the pool table room.

Lower section of the bar antique medallion.

I'm sure it is no surprise to you that we decided on a French and German theme. We began with the game room/theatre area. Since I have an obsession with accenting ceilings, we created a ceiling with whitewashed beadboard and dark gray beams. We decided on painting the upper part of the walls Light French Gray by *Sherwin Williams*. We added a chair rail and white beadboard on the lower section of the wall in the bar area. We included my husband's family sofa, antiques, and modern accents. Notice my ping pong table sits on the pool table perfectly. Antique French wooden doors with glass accent the transition from the pool room to the bar area and wine cellar area. Two black iron matching ceiling light fixtures from *Progressive Lighting* set the mood for carefree games and avid sport enthusiasts.

The wine bar includes Gary's collection of Tobies and our family memorabilia. Surprisingly, the base for our bar was an original rough, worn workbench. We sanded and stained the surface and added trim. The challenging transformation was accomplished with the use of the mahogany carved wood from our former upright piano. The finish of the wood gave the shelving and backdrop an incredibly imitable appearance. An antique gilded gold medallion accents the base of the bar. The area has a subtle and sophisticated ambience of a pub in France or Germany.

The eighteenth-century antique armoire, personal collectables, refreshments,
and music set the scene for an evening of merriment for all.

Section 3
Mind-Blowing Classic Tudor and Craftsman Homes

The living room of my client Bob's original home, which we staged

The joy of being a designer is that every home is a unique personal story. The designer helps clients' enhance their visions of their dream homes. The process is invigorating, surprising, and inspiring, similar to going to a play. There is unexpected tension, transformations, and shared discoveries when plotting the interior and exterior settings. The rewards are endless!

At times, I meet a new client merely by coincidence. I was taking a walk in my neighborhood and observed a woman sitting in her car. She was peering intently at a neighborhood residence. As I walked by, we introduced ourselves. Jennifer told me that she was waiting for her real estate agent to finish showing her home that had been on the market for some time. She called me a few days later to request that I stage her home for sale.

The house had great bones. Jennifer and I selected paint and enjoyed shopping together to refine her home. We purchased accessories and a few pieces of furniture as well as removed unnecessary items. The timeless mix of modern and traditional styles transformed the home into a cozy, welcoming space. Fortunately, the house sold a few days after staging.

Jennifer referred me to her father Bob, who was selling his home nearby. He was relocating to a newly purchased home to be near Jennifer and her family. Bob had a successful background in architectural building.

His original home was large with exquisite architectural features, yet it required some staging. In retrospect, it needed only minor renovations, painting, accessorizing, and removal of unnecessary items to prepare the residence for a substantial sale. His design style was traditional with a modern mix and personal twist. He had a beautiful grand piano and other classic furnishings to enhance the sale.

I was impressed with his new home selection: a classical craftsman architectural style home. We started our design adventure with memorable shopping trips that took us to antique, modern, and consignment stores for an entire year. We sought items that reflected the new home's character and Bob's lifestyle. His interests were family, aviation, cars, art, history, and architectural elements. These combined in the creation of a masculine home that reflected his lively personality and transformed the new home from bland to grand.

Bob and I planned the flow of the rooms by space planning, renovation of the outdated kitchen, and widening of the hallway entrance. We selected paints, furniture, and accessories, and requisitioned bold colorful textures to enrich the neutral pallet of white, navy, and hues of gray.

The transformations of Jennifer's and Bob's homes are beyond spectacular!

PART 1

The Tudor Home Kitchen Makeover—*du Petit au Grand*

After Jennifer was settled in her new home, she told me she was renovating the kitchen with the help of her husband Latham and father Bob. I was fortunate to consult with them during the renovation. To say the least, the family is overjoyed with their striking new kitchen.

Jennifer's new Tudor-style home

The kitchen make-over was a miraculous evolution! The original plan had only an arched doorway between the kitchen and small eating area. After renovation, her petite, segmented kitchen was transformed into a fantastic, functional, family friendly kitchen.

The following pictures depict the stages of the construction and redesign process of Jennifer's kitchen project.

We opened the main dividing wall and crafted an accompanying arch that is higher than the doorway arch to give the room a sense of height and openness.

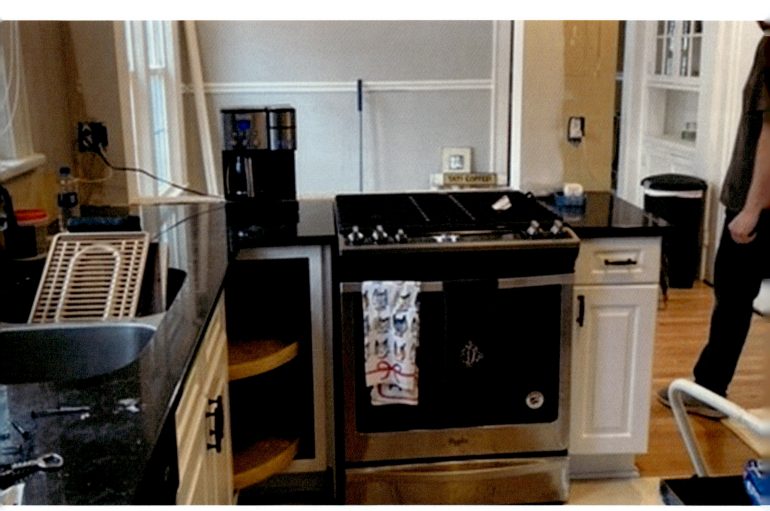

White painted cabinets, Lazy Susan corner cabinet, hardware, and black granite were added to the space.

The cat is protective of its new kitchen! The refrigerator was moved to the original laundry room. The washer and dryer were relocated to the hallway.

The extension of the new black granite countertop from *G & C*, Dallas, Georgia makes the kitchen user friendly and is perfect for entertaining.

Jennifer and friend Elizabeth shopped and added accessories for the hutch as well as the family feline.

Terrific outcome. I love the lighting, bench, and bar stools! Secretly, I wish I could have the life of Jennifer's cat.

PART 2

The Classic Craftsman Home—One of the Most Popular Home Styles in America

I was thankful that Jennifer referred me to her father. Bob was an auspicious owner of an architectural metal cladding company. Initially, we worked on staging his home to sell. Then we blended our design experiences with decisions accented with intuition and a pinch of reinvention to design his new home. We compared products, considered his interests and his relaxed, sophisticated style. Subsequently, we celebrated the resulting artistic, yet functional, transitional design in his new historical home.

Staging Success—A Moving Experience

Bob's gorgeous home he was selling in my subdivision. Some rooms required updating, rearranging, and painting. There was a need for repurposing, modernizing, and removal of furnishings. Bob expressed his preference for a design style that emanated a modern twist to vintage furnishings.

Bob's living room in the home that he sold.

Before picture of the dining room prior to staging.

After staging picture of Bob's dining room. Lantern and candelabras
are from *Linen and Flax*, Roswell, Georgia.

The Renovation of the New Craftsman Home—A Mix of Vintage and Modern Elements

Entrance to Bob's new Sears 1910 Craftsman home. Gustav Stickley's Architects for the homes include Charles and Henry Greene from California and Harvey Ellis from Syracuse.

Bob and I were determined to maintain the architectural features of the craftsman home. We searched for sophisticated designs and unique items to enliven the spaces. Focusing on a harmonious flow of design from one room to another allowed for a spacious, yet cozy representation of his life. This was accomplished by initiating space planning as well as selecting contrasting yet coordinating elements. We included bold textures and elegant lighting that were tantamount to the color scheme.

118

Vive la différence

The Main Floor Hallway—Memorable Personalized Design

Bob's renovated hallway that was originally nondescript. The stair wall
features pictures of his aviation experiences and collections.

Bob's hallway features original modern art, Downtown Mixed Media by Charles Ross purchased from *Huff and Harrington Art,* Atlanta. The crystal accessories are from *10-10 Thrift*, Douglasville, Georgia. We added an antique Oriental rug for a classic effect.

The Family Room—Sophistication and Comfort at its Best

After picture of Bob's main floor hallway with a glimpse of the renovated family room.

Bob's renovated family room. We purchased the sofa from *Lazy Boy*, the rug from *Jaipur*, leather ottoman from *Gabby's*, and the mirrors and chandelier from *West Side Market*.

Bob's two mirrors hung horizontally form a lasting impression and accent the beautiful chandelier. Definitely wow factors for the room!

The Living Room—Focus on the Historical Architectural Features of a Space

View from Bob's hallway to renovated living room and adjoining dining room. New flooring from *Floor Works*, Dallas, Georgia.

Bob's living room and dining room including a newly purchased antique oriental rug and accessories. The home's architectural details represent craftsmanship classic style at its best.

Bob's coiffured ceiling in his living room with dark gray beams and *Sherwin Williams's* Light French Gray paint.

Bob's peaceful and sophisticated window seat area. *Kravet Couture* fabric, Modern Ottoman Silver.

Music and wine anyone? Bob's music room is located off the living room. *Sherwin Williams's* Classic French paint provides depth to the room. The dramatic chaise lounge fabric was purchased at *Forsyth Fabric*, Atlanta. The gorgeous candlesticks are from *Historic Roswell Antiques and Interiors*, Roswell, Georgia.

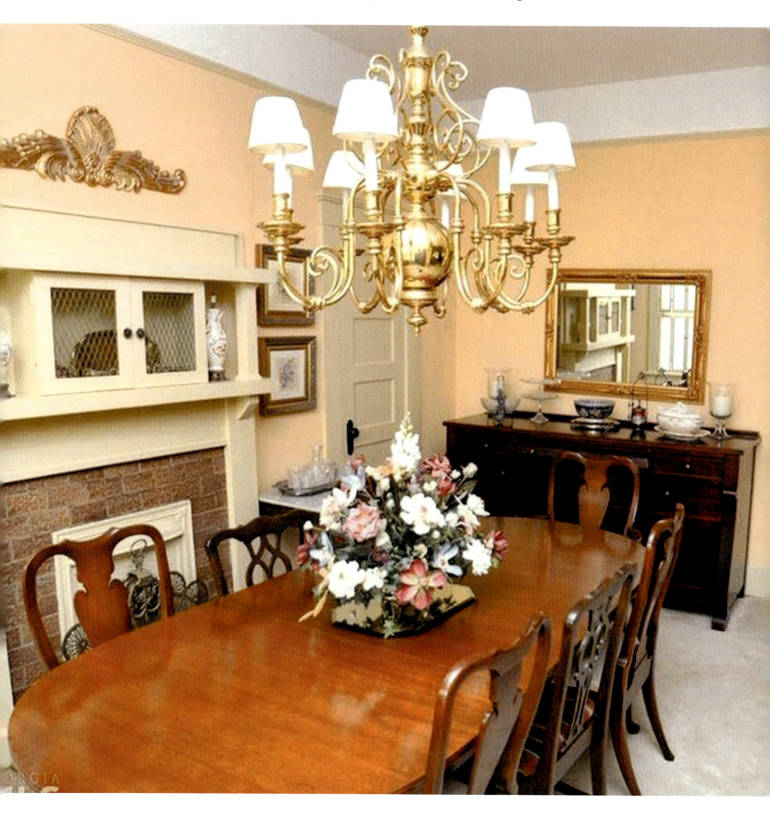

Before picture of Bob's dining room in the new home

After (next page) picture of Bob's striking dining room. Fabric and silk wallpaper are from Schumacher, Felicity Sapphire Quiet Beauty Collection.

Before Kitchen renovation pictures.

Transition from dining room to kitchen. Bob's fabulous original modern art, *Papillion* by *Augusta Wilson,* in his renovated kitchen. It was purchased from *Huff and Harrington Gallery*, Atlanta. The art wall in the kitchen was painted In the Navy by *Sherwin Williams*.

After picture Bob's striking, renovated kitchen. The floor and backsplash tile are from *Tile and Stone*, Douglasville, Georgia. The granite countertop is from *G&C,* Dallas, Georgia. Under-counter lighting illuminates the kitchen tile.

Bob loves technology and sustainability. He uses eco-friendly sky lights, lighting, natural finishes, and enjoys *Alexa Voice* for his appliances.

Mixing different tiles with granite or other materials is like playing a game of chess.

The original art and magnificent island with storage makes the kitchen functional as well as spectacular.

Kitchen with eco-friendly skylights and functional pot rack from *William and Sonoma*. The energy efficient range hood is from *KOBE*.

Believe me, when the kitchen was finished, we all celebrated with a glass of wine.

Bob's kitchen plans.

The Powder Room—Playful Nautical Theme

Bob's renovated main floor half bathroom conveniently located near the back entry to the swimming pool area. "Unsinkable" fish wallpaper purchased at *Wallpaper and Stuff*, Smyrna, Georgia.

Screened—In Front Porch—A Calming Retreat

Escape time! Bob's wrap-around front porch.

Petit à petit l'oiseau fait son nid! It takes patience and perseverance when designing a home that favors the life of the owner, but it sure is worth it.

Due to my design experiences, I agree with the notion that the French don't give up easily!

137

Section 4

A Facelift for Two Condos in Atlanta: Intriguing Adventures in Design!

PART 1

Downtown Condo Great Room: Great Bones for Design Transformation

I'm always on the hunt for opportunities to design remarkable spaces. The owner of a fantastic property in downtown Atlanta contacted me after visiting Bob's craftsman home. He raved about Bob's dining room and asked me to decorate a condo he purchased years ago. The condo's "draw" was the large front-facing windows and fireplace, the metro downtown location, convenience to stores, plus the restaurants, theatre and nearby university events.

My Challenge: The client wanted everything to be from Consignment type stores!

The story: The condo was completely empty and painted in hues of gray. The floors were all hardwood and the bathrooms and closets had been updated. My client did not want to remove walls even though the kitchen was small. The design plan was to accessorize and create a transitional style home.

First steps of the challenge: The client and I earnestly began our search for sophisticated yet functional, modern, and classic style furnishings. We kept an open mind for special finds that would provide capricious touches.

We valued the idea of buying consignment high-end classic furnishings. The hunt for the living room furnishings began with a visit to the *Sarah Cyrus Home* consignment shop in Atlanta. As my client drove up in his gorgeous Jaguar, I pondered why he only wanted to shop at consignment and discount shops. Maybe he was wiser than most.

We shared our priorities for shopping. Then the quest began!

We realized that a sofa was the essential item that should be one of our first purchases. Fortunately, we came upon a *Bernhardt* sofa in a neutral color that was perfect for the living room. As my client sat comfortably on the sofa, he saw an eye-catching slipper chair with sleek lines. We were told it was found at the *Atlanta Decorative Arts Center* (ADAC), known for impeccable furnishings. We realized that the chair's modern sleekness would complement the ambience of the living room as well as serve as a conversation piece. We noticed a quality *Hooker* furniture chair. It coordinated with the sofa and was in excellent shape. Purchased!

At that time, the client asked me to follow him to another space in the store. He was impressed with an oil painting in a gilded frame that portrayed a colorful water scene. The painting became the inspiration for the condo's color scheme to blend the other design elements of form, pattern, and texture to create harmony throughout the space. We felt certain that the painting would look fabulous above the sofa.

Success!

Second Steps of the Challenge: Persistence! It was time for online consignment and discount shopping for the two bedrooms and remaining furnishings for the living room, dining area, and kitchen. We searched endless online consignment sites, wholesale, and antique stores.

I persistently explored consignment stores in the Atlanta area. In particular, I went to the *Board of Trade* in Roswell, Georgia. I arrived at the right time! I found matching dining room chairs in subtle colors at an unbelievable price my client loved.

By the way, the store had a section with women's vintage clothing. I thought to myself, *Consignment shopping can be rewarding in more ways than one!*

After all, Karl Lagerfeld said it well: "We need houses as we need clothes, architecture stimulates fashion. It's like hunger and thirst—you need them both."[5]

I shopped at *Antiques and Beyond* antique mall and *Westside Market* in Atlanta where I often found great furniture and accessories. I visited *Ben's Antiques* in Douglasville, Georgia where I discovered a gorgeous inlaid Louis XV vintage desk for the living room.

Back online, my client unearthed a *Hickory* furniture sofa table and a variety of vintage bedroom furnishings. Instinctively, I searched online for stores like *Groupon, Pillow Fever,* and *Home Goods* as I purchased bedding, rugs, and unique accessories that related to my client's hobbies, color choices, and desires.

Unequivocally, I was truly enjoying the challenge.

Further Steps of the Challenge: We were up to the challenge when we stopped at the unique *Thrift 10-10* in Douglasville, Georgia. The owner shops on occasion at AmericasMart and donates proceeds to charity. We discovered the perfect sized circular wood dining table, and accompanying large arched mirror for his dining area. We celebrated when we found two fabulous lamps and a bench for the master bedroom. A great shopping spree for a good cause!

As I look back upon the consignment challenge, the shopping exercises were as good as or better than working out. It is living proof that consignment and discount shopping pays off.

Before picture of condo great room

Picture of the open concept main great room of the condo after renovation. I love the modern feeling of the intimate dining space with the table and arched mirror from the *10-10 Thrift Store, Douglasville, Georgia* that provides depth for the room. The two matching dining chairs are from *The Board of Trade*, Roswell, Georgia. The modern slipper chair from the Atlanta Decorative Arts Center was purchased from *Sarah Cyrus Home, Atlanta*.

The living room came alive with the colorful pillows from Pier One. They complement the colors in the oil painting purchased at *Sarah Cyrus Home,* Atlanta. The wood floors are accented by a sophisticated, timeless rug and the vintage Hickory Chair coffee table we found online.

> Sidebar: As a designer, I often prefer a neutral color for a sofa since it provides opportunities to change color schemes in rooms. Pillows and accessories can be easily changed to bring a "new room" feeling to a space. By the way, I confess that I have a pillow fetish!

There is no doubt that details make a huge impact on design. The Louis XV desk from *Ben's Antiques* makes a wow statement with the mix of furnishings in the living room. The substantial furnishings are vintage and modern timeless pieces, as evidenced in the *Bernhardt* sofa, and *Hooker* chair.

Hooker chair in excellent condition. Great find! A unique ADAC slipper chair
Both chairs purchased at *Sarah Cyrus Home, Atlanta.*

Lessons Learned in the Life of a Designer: You too can become
a connoisseur of consignment and discount shops. The bottom line
is that you don't need to spend a fortune to create great design.

PART 2

Exclusive Condo in Vinings, Georgia: A Dining Area Revival

A real estate friend, Debbie, asked me to stage a condo that had been on the market for some time. It is located in upscale Vinings, Georgia. My first thought was why not design a space that buyers would find unforgettable? Originally, the dining space off the kitchen was utilized as a family room. I decided to relocate the small dining area from the corner of the spacious living room and create a dining space in the kitchen area. During the hunt for furnishings for the dining area, I was thrilled to discover a rectangular wood trestle table with a herringbone surface. It turned out to be the perfect choice for the space. Blending a mix of accessories, greenery, and colorful modern art, added touches of contemporary style to the neutral color palate of the room.

Buyers appreciated the idea that the dramatic wingback chairs could flank the ends of the table or be used at a sitting area by the large window with a picturesque view of the serene woods.

I love that the kitchen feels more spacious and intimate due to placement of the room
furnishings. The wine bar cart is from *World Market*. Chairs from *Pier One*.
Fortunately, the dining area staging was memorable and the condo sold quickly. The buyers loved
the furnishing and purchased the trestle table, chairs, bar cart, and some of the accessories.

When staging, I remind myself,
Paris ne s'est pas fait en un jour—
Paris was not built in a day!

Section 5

Heart-Stirring Transitional Model and Spec Homes

It was a beautiful, memorable day. I was in a great state of mind after meeting with one of my favorite clients. I leisurely decided to drive through the location near my former interior design store since the area was expanding rapidly.

It was by happenstance that I was drawn into an unrivaled new subdivision, Estates at Cornerstone, in Powder Springs, Georgia. After driving through the subdivision I could sense the essence of the timeless, sophisticated architectural and design style of the area. I had an overwhelming desire to collaborate in a design endeavor with the builder.

It was as if it was meant to be. I decided to see if the builder was available. I spotted the sales office. As I walked toward the edifice the builder, Jennifer Blomquist simultaneously exited the sales office.

I noticed that Jennifer was in a hurry, but took time to talk with me. I introduced myself and mentioned that she must be the builder; she responded with a smile. I explained that I was an interior designer who enjoyed working with builders. We clicked immediately. Jennifer indicated that she needed assistance with design for the model and spec homes. In that moment, I knew we would be working together; what I did not know was the foreshadowing of a lasting friendship.

Soon after, we talked and she hired me. I learned a great deal from her building experience as well as her design skills. I followed her lead as I avidly selected exterior and interior finishes for model and spec homes. I was fortunate to work with her in another of her subdivisions, Somerset Oaks.

She provided humor, wisdom, and creative suggestions for sophisticated and comfortable homes that portray unexpected elegant features. She had a sense of combining history, personal touches, and lasting features to her homes. I am forever thankful for this fantastic collaboration. I can see why she was honored as a promising builder in the *Atlantan* magazine.

The pictures in this section are mainly from our combined efforts. I included Model Home One that Jennifer designed prior to our time together.

It was *coup de foudre*—love at first sight! One of the Blomquist homes with breathtaking views at the top of Lost Mountain (elevation 1,211 feet) from the Estates at Cornerstone subdivision.

View of the open concept living room and kitchen in Model Home One.

PART I

Model Home One at the Top of Lost Mountain: Estates at Cornerstone Subdivision

Powder Springs, Georgia

The living room of Model Home One. My design center for the subdivision was located in the lower level of the home.

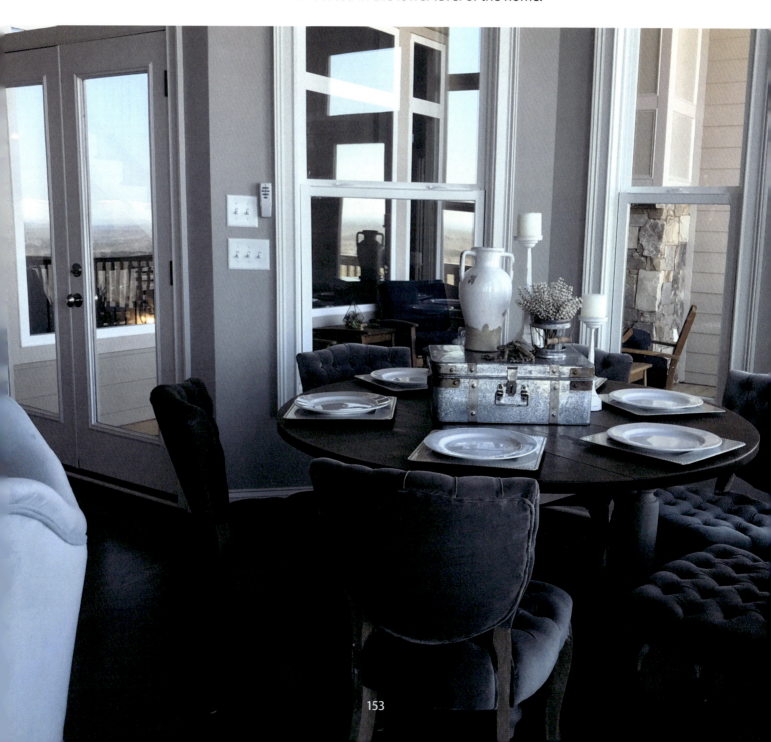

Nothing but the best! Timeless backsplash, modern hardware, functionality, durability, and upscale appliances are featured in Model Home One.

The dining room gives a sense of relaxation and sophistication as it welcomes
lively conversations. It is located off the entry hall of Model Home One.

A heavenly view from the serene master bedroom in Model Home One in the Estates at Cornerstone.

I love this luxurious master bathroom in Model Home One! It features flooring with the herringbone pattern, elegant lighting, high end hardware, and a beautiful wood barn door. What could be better?

Another peek at the master bathroom details in Model Home One at the Estates at Cornerstone.

Model Home Two in the Estates at Cornerstone Subdivision

Notice the mix of different finishes on the home.

You undoubtedly guessed that I love this ceiling! The kitchen and family room in Model Home Two feature hardwood floors, transitional beautiful tile, and furnishings. The kitchen has an open concept and adjoins the dining area. The table top is durable stainless steel and is from *Westside Market*, Atlanta.

No doubt about it: ceilings can make dramatic impressions. You can't help but notice that the dining room in Model Home Two has over-the-top architectural details.

A view of the bookshelves in Model Home Two with a herringbone pattern and floor to ceiling tiled fireplace. Furniture from *Westside Market*, Atlanta.

PART 3

Model Home in Somerset Oaks Subdivision, Powder Springs, Georgia

The Model Home located in Somerset Oaks subdivision.
Love the *Sherwin Williams* white paint with Caviar black paint trim on the exterior plus the stone wall, batten-board siding effects, three car garage, and grand porch with multiple French doors.

The Model Home in Somerset Oaks has a magnetic draw due to its cozy and sophisticated style. It is a "feel good" space. The stacked brick fireplace, shiplap, and white bookshelves provide a great focal point and gathering place for family and friends.

Exterior meets interior! High impact overview of the living room, windmill fan, shiplap above the fireplace to the ceiling, ceiling beam stained the same as the railing, and view of the exterior deck in the Model Home at Somerset Oaks.

I love the fabulous kitchen in the Model Home at Somerset Oaks with the mixture of textures, details, navy blue island base and range hood, lighting, wood accents, and white tile and quartz countertops. Lighting from *Lighting Works*, Dallas, Georgia. The kitchen is welcoming and functional. The combination is conducive to perfect entertaining. Time for some *somptueux* chocolate soufflé!

The exceptional kitchen and dining or keeping/dining area in the Model Home at Somerset Oaks has a beamed ceiling that leads your eye to the tree-lined outdoors.

If you love tranquility, the master bath at the Model Home fulfills your dreams! Tile from *Interceramic Tile and Stone Gallery*, Kennesaw, Georgia. The fabulous soaking tub calls for a relaxing escape from reality and a glass of vintage French wine.

PART 4

Additional Spaces in Spec Homes: Design Collaboration

A spec home Master Bath at Somerset Oaks featuring a waterfall tile in the shower.

A close-up of the spec home shower with waterfall tile and a mix of tile finishes. The tile from *Interceramic Tile* in the Atlanta area.

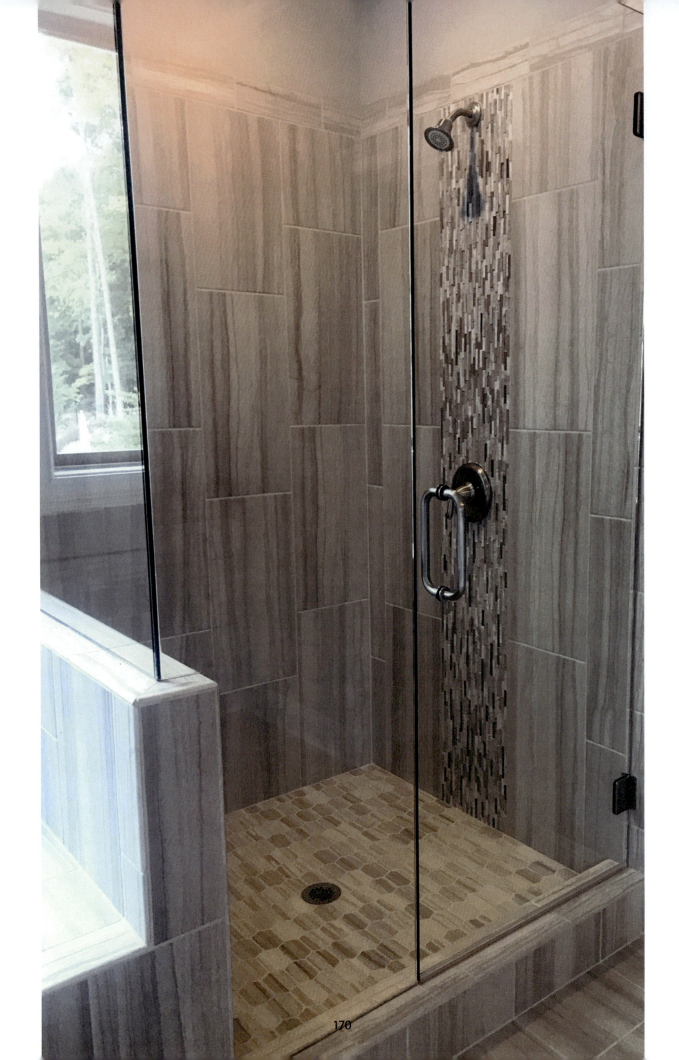

170

This appealing open kitchen features durable and beautiful hardwood floors, white cabinets, and a wood island with state-of the-art appliances and lighting.

Elizabeth's historic home

Section 6

A Memorable Historical Home: A Touch of France

In my world of interior design, renovating a home over a period of time can lead to lifelong "design soulmates," such as client Elizabeth and myself.

I met Elizabeth through my terrific clients Jennifer and Bob. During Bob's home renovation, Elizabeth, his next door neighbor, dropped by to see how his redesign was progressing. My first impression was that Elizabeth had a wealth of information about historical homes at her fingertips. I listened attentively to her comments about preserving historical features since I could relate to her experiences. As you know, I previously decorated my former historical home in New York.

Fundamentally, we agree that a home's design must be family functional, aesthetically appropriate, beautiful, and symmetrical yet surprisingly imperfect at times, especially when you have two active teenage boys like Elizabeth. We confided in each other that good design can be a *de'fi a'livrer*—a challenge to deliver. We were determined to include a touch of France as well as European influences. In retrospect, we agreed that it takes resourcefulness to pull a historic home together for *la famille* in today's world.

French design "its artistry, it's attitude, it's style...a mix of panache and simplicity,
taste and resourcefulness that is at once inviting, surprising, and inspiring."[6]
—Betty Lou Phillips

Initially, we decorated her living and dining rooms as we worked around the teenagers' computers, internet gadgets, and desire to live casually, yet no challenge was too big to prevent us from our design mission.

Elizabeth's discerning design style is all about sophistication, subtle yet vibrant luxury, and comfort for her family home. We agree that shopping is the best therapy. Not to mention, we always started each shopping spree with a stop at Starbucks.

Our adventures included buying trips to *Antiques and Beyond Antique Mall, Cobb Antique Mall, Westside Market, Ballard Design, Forsyth, Lewis and Sheron, Curtain Exchange, ADAC, The Romo Group,* textiles from *Brunschwig & Fil, Kravet, Lee Jofa, Boxwoods, Pottery Barn, Lamp Arts Inc.,* and *Americas Mart* in Atlanta.

Consequently, Elizabeth's *Magnifique* home embodies our efforts to reflect her blended design style and accommodate her family's lifestyle.

"There is something eye-catching about contrasts, as well as continuity".
—Suzanne Kasler, Designer[7]

Could it be an obsession? As design soulmates, we can't wait to work on her next room together.

The Entrance: Historical Grand Entrance Hall

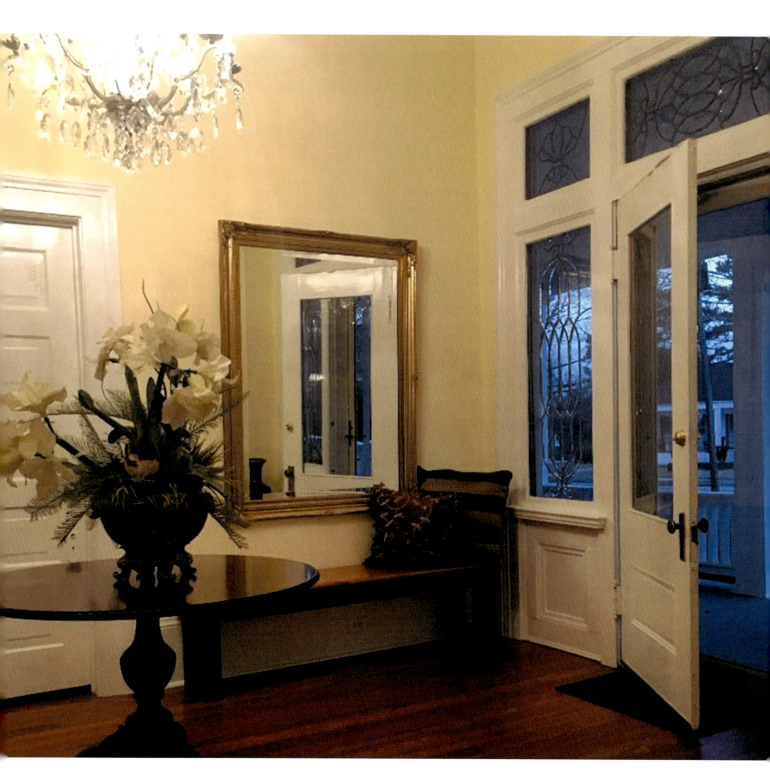

Welcome to Elizabeth's entrance hall! Walls are *Porter Paint*, Banana Pudding.

Elizabeth's marble top console we had painted with *Sherwin Williams* Perfect Greige paint.

Elizabeth's entrance hall antique chair new fabric from *Lewis and Sheron* in Atlanta.

Before Picture antique chair.

After Picture antique chair.

The Living Room: Bright and airy atmosphere

Picture of the teen influenced living room: A work in progress. Elizabeth's new slipcovered sofa and rug are from *Ballard Designs*; *Bernhardt* console table, lamp and chairs from *Westside Market* in Atlanta.

Living room rug from *Ballard Designs*.

The Dining Room: French-style setting

The dining room bay window area wallpaper from *The Romo Group* Black edition,
Xanthina Wallcovering collection—"Eden Daffodil" discovered at ADAC in Atlanta.

The gorgeous wallpaper is only in the bay window area of the dining room. The silk draperies from *The Curtain Exchange* in Atlanta are trimmed in blue and lined with an inner liner for a graceful puddled effect. The draperies and furniture add symmetry to the sitting area in Elizabeth's dining room. The reupholstered blue chairs, French stool, altar table from Westside Market, Atlanta are wow factors for the space.

New antique porcelain statue of Shakespeare and French style console table from *Antiques and Beyond Antique Mall*, Dazzling glass candle holders from *Boxwoods* in Atlanta.
Shakespeare quotation—was he pondering great design?
"See first that the design is wise and just: that ascertained, pursue it resolutely;
do not for one repulse forego the purpose that you resolved to effect."

Before picture of the dining room buffet.

After picture of the dining room new faux painted French style buffet.

The Master Bedroom: It's all about details! A mix of textiles and accessories create a mood of comfortable elegance.

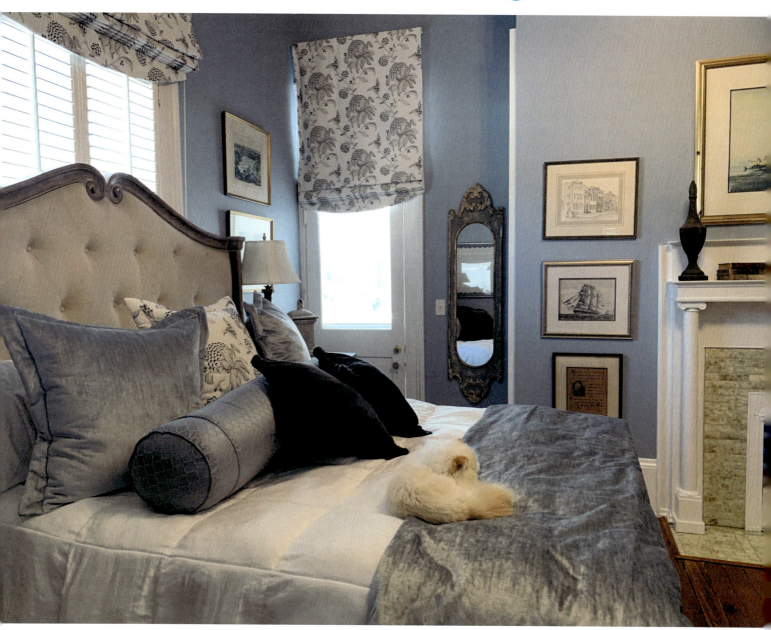

Master bedroom with French influences after renovation. Bedside lamps are from *Cobb Antique Mall*, Marietta, Georgia. A mix of *Brunschwig & Fi*, *Lee Jofa*, and *Kravet* fabrics make for a luxurious sleep.

Another view of the serene master bedroom. Accessories from *Boxwoods* in Atlanta and Elizabeth's collection of vintage art, some from France.

The Kitchen: Lively blue and white design

The sitting area in the kitchen invites conversation. Wingback chairs, un-skirted after reupholstering. Table from *Cobb Antique Mall*, Marietta, Georgia.

The kitchen sitting area chairs skirted. **Before** re-upholstery by *Silas Turpin Upholstery*.

The Power of Details: Contrasting elements of design

Elizabeth's new pillows for her entrance hall bench from *Ballard Design*.

Elizabeth's dining room metal table dazzling accessory from *Ballard Designs*.

Elizabeth's living room wingback chairs pillow from *Ballard Designs*.

Elizabeth's half-bath wallpaper by *Cole and Son, purchased from Wallpaper and Stuff, Smyrna, Georgia.*

He appreciates a deep kitchen sink and quartz countertops.

Section 7

Fine Design, Wine, and a Celebrity Chef's French Recipe Choices

Chef Scott on *The Kelly Clarkson Show*

C'est vraiment très bon when you combine fine wine and design with scrumptious French recipes. This is especially true when featuring suggestions from celebrity Chef Scott from San Antonio. Chef Scott is known for his humor, expertise, television appearances, and international travel to restaurants where he collaborates with celebrity chefs.

Chef Scott appreciates the importance of a bright, open concept design for a kitchen and adjoining family room, dining, or keeping room. He values multiple working spaces with plenty of counter space. A large pantry is invaluable to him.

Chef Scott and wife Lauren's family kitchen.

Chef Scott enjoys a butcher block stainless steel island with a large assortment of pans. He likes the functionality of a pot filler faucet over a gas range plus a double oven.

Client and friend Liz's living room is the center of attention when guests meet for drinks and appetizers.

THE CHEF'S FRENCH RECIPE CHOICES

Appetizers, Sides, and Salads

Rustic Dijon and Dill Vinaigrette
(Serves 8)

Ingredients

2 tablespoons Grey Poupon Country Dijon Mustard

2 cloves of garlic, minced or zested, approximately 1/4 ounce

1 large Davidson's Safest Choice Large Pasteurized Shell Egg, 1 egg yolk only, white discarded

1/4 cup red wine vinegar

2 tablespoons fresh dill, minced or finely chopped

1 1/4 cups extra virgin olive oil

Instructions

1. In a bowl, whisk together Dijon, garlic, and egg yolk. Whisk until mixture is light in color and well emulsified.
2. Add red wine vinegar and dill. Whisk again to incorporate.
3. While whisking, slowly add oil to form a loose emulsion. Season to taste with cracked pepper and salt as needed.
4. Place into a container with a tight-fitting lid and refrigerate for at least 30 minutes to allow flavors to meld.
5. Serve on salad or over grilled chicken and shrimp. Dressing will keep up to 3 days in refrigeration.

The kitchen pass-through accentuates the ease of entertaining in Liz's home.

Fresh Lemon-Braised Leeks

(Serves 4)

Ingredients

6 tablespoons Plugra European Style Unsalted Butter, divided use, half for sautéing and remainder for finishing.

3 tablespoons extra virgin olive oil

2 pounds leeks, approximately 6 stalks

4 sprigs of fresh thyme

2 tablespoons white wine vinegar

1 1/4 cups chicken stock

1 tablespoon fresh chives, chopped small, plus more as needed for garnishing

Instructions

1. Regarding leeks: remove green tops of leeks entirely. Trim roots at tip but leave root intact so leeks stay together when cooking. Once trimmed, cut in half and remove any tougher outer leaves.
2. Place a medium sized stainless steel or non-stick skillet with a tight fitting lid over medium high heat.
3. Add butter and oil and allow to melt and for butter to get bubbly before adding in leeks cut side down and thyme sprigs.
4. 4. Season leeks liberally with salt and pepper and allow to cook for approximately 10 minutes before flipping. Leeks should be slightly browned before flipping.
5. Once leeks are flipped, cook 5 more minutes before adding white wine vinegar. Cook until vinegar is evaporated then add remaining butter and stock.
6. Bring everything to a rapid simmer, then cover and reduce heat to low. Allow to cook for approximately 30 to 40 minutes or until leeks are very tender.
7. Serve leeks with any remaining pan juices and garnish with chopped chives.

Main Course

Fabulous design in Gail and Neal's dining room. A place to share a
glass of wine and enjoy the main course with friends!

Steak Frites
(Serves 2)

Ingredients

1 1/2 pounds organic russet potatoes, washed and peeled

2 quarts canola or peanut oil, more as needed for frying, plus 1 to 2 tablespoons for brushing over steaks

4 ounces beef tenderloin filet mignon, 2 filets

2 teaspoons True Texas BBQ Salt and Pepper Blend, or as needed for seasoning steaks

4 tablespoons Plugra European Style Unsalted Butter, plus more as needed

4 sprigs of fresh thyme, 3 to 5 sprigs approximately 1/4 to 1/2 ounce

Instructions

1. Cut peeled potatoes into fries with French fry cutter or by hand into even sticks. Bring a large pot of water to a boil then add fries.
2. Allow fries to cook for 6 minutes, then drain off water. Place fries into a bowl and rinse with cold water until water runs clear and starch is mostly washed off. Set aside and pat dry.
3. Place oil into a large Dutch oven and set over medium heat. Bring oil to 350° F. Adjust heat as needed to maintain temp by raising or lowering temperature.
4. While par-cooked fries are rinsing, place a cast iron skillet over medium heat. Allow to get very hot.
5. Season each filet liberally on both sides with salt and pepper. Add a little reserved oil to the top of each steak and place meat into hot pan.
6. Allow steaks to sear for 4 to 6 minutes, flip steaks, and add butter and thyme sprigs. While steaks are cooking, brush or baste tops of steaks with melted butter.
7. While steaks are cooking, fry French fries in batches until golden brown and crispy. Remove finished fries to a sheet pan fitted with a wire rack to drain, and season liberally with salt.
8. Cook steaks until desired doneness is reached, allowing them to rest.
9. Serve steak with fries and spoon any remaining pan juices over steak and fries if desired. Season to taste.

Confit Chicken Thighs with Orange and Thyme

(Serves 8)

Ingredients

3 pounds boneless skinless chicken thighs

1 large navel orange, thinly sliced, approximately 8 ounces

8 sprigs of fresh thyme, plus more as needed

3 cups Rustico di Casa Asaro Olio Nuovo Extra Virgin Olive Oil, as needed for covering chicken

Instructions

1. Preheat oven to 325° F.
2. Season chicken thighs liberally with salt and pepper or your favorite rub.
3. Place chicken thighs into an oven safe pot with a tight fitting lid. Arrange sliced oranges evenly over chicken and add fresh thyme.
4. Add enough olive oil to just cover chicken, approximately 2 to 3 cups. Cover pot with lid and place in the oven.
5. Cook for 45 to 60 minutes or until the chicken is fully cooked and is falling apart tender.
6. Remove chicken from olive oil; discard oranges and thyme. Serve chicken over rice or pasta and garnish with fresh herbs.
7. Chef's Note: Reserve a little leftover oil and use for adding to rice or pasta for extra flavor.

Desserts

Scrumptious Pate Choux Dough Recipe.

Pate Choux Dough
(serves 24)

Ingredients

6 ounces Plugra European Style Unsalted Butter, 1 1/2 sticks, cut into thin pads

1 cup water

1 cup whole milk

1 teaspoon kosher salt

3 tablespoons granulated sugar

2 cups all-purpose flour

8 large eggs

Instructions

1. Preheat oven to 425° F.
2. In a medium sized pot, add butter, water, milk, salt, and sugar, Bring to a boil, being careful to monitor so it doesn't boil over. Adjust heat as necessary.
3. Turn heat down to low and add flour to the milk mixture. Whisk vigorously for 2 to 3 minutes until it forms a wet dough and begins to leave a film in the pot. Remove from heat and allow to cool slightly.
4. Add slightly cooled dough to a stand mixer fitted with paddle attachment.
5. Turn mixer on to low speed and mix dough until all steam is gone and dough cools slightly, approximately 8 to 10 minutes.
6. Gradually add eggs 1 or 2 at a time, allowing eggs to incorporate into dough before each addition. Once eggs are incorporated, turn mixer to higher speed for 1 minute to allow dough to get fluffy.
7. Remove dough to a piping bag or a gallon zip top bag. Pipe golf ball sized rolls (or larger if preferred) onto a sheet pan fitted with parchment paper. Pipe balls approximately 1 to 2 inches apart.
8. Bake until puffed up and starting to brown slightly on top, approximately 20 to 25 minutes.
9. Rotate pan then turn heat down to 350° F and bake another 15 to 25 minutes or until nicely golden brown and set.

French Madeleines
(Serves 24)

Ingredients

4 large eggs

1 teaspoon lemon zest

2/3 cup granulated sugar

2 teaspoons vanilla extract

1 1/2 cups all-purpose flour

1 teaspoon baking powder

1 teaspoon kosher or sea salt

8 ounces Plugra European Style Unsalted Butter, melted and set aside, butter should still be warm

Instructions

1. In a bowl, whisk together eggs, lemon zest, sugar, and vanilla extract until creamy and sugar is mostly dissolved; set aside.
2. In a separate bowl, sift together flour, baking powder, and salt.
3. Add warm melted butter and egg mixture to flour and whisk until batter just comes together and is smooth.
4. Place a piece of plastic wrap over the batter surface to keep a skin from forming. Place another sheet of plastic wrap over the entire bowl and refrigerate overnight or at least 8 hours (24 hours will yield the best results).
5. Preheat oven to 375º F. Spray a madeleine pan with non-stick spray.
6. Scoop approximately an ounce of batter evenly into each mold.
7. Bake 10 to 15 minutes or until madeleines are just lightly browned and puffed up.
8. Allow madeleines to cool slightly in pan before transferring to a serving basket. Serve while still warm.
9. Chef's Note: These make a great appetizer paired with Rosé wine for any party.

Fresh Lemon Chantilly
(Serves 10)

Ingredients

2 cups heavy whipping cream

1/8 teaspoon kosher or sea salt

1 large lemon, skin only, peeled into strips

1 teaspoon vanilla bean paste

1/3 cup powdered sugar, plus more as needed for sweetness

Instructions

1. In a plastic container or jar with a tight fitting lid, add cold whipping cream, salt, and lemon peels.
2. Stir with a spoon and place lid on tightly. Refrigerate overnight or at least 8 hours.
3. When ready to use, stir cream mixture with a spoon then strain out all lemon peels and discard.
4. Place strained cream into a bowl along with vanilla bean paste and powdered sugar.
5. Whip by hand or using a hand mixer until stiff peaks form. Refrigerate until ready to use.
6. Serve over fruit or over warm pies or pastries.

The French are not known as frequent sweet wine drinkers. However, France's Sauternes wine from the southwest region of Bordeaux are a great choice for after-dinner wine and more.

Elaine's French wine choice to help you unwind at the end of the day: if you like red wine when dining, you could try my Drouillard ancestor's wine from Chateau Lynch-Bages Pauillac in France https://www.thewinecellarinsider.com/bordeaux-wine-producer-profiles/bordeaux/pauillac/lynch-bages/

Section 8

Lux Living on the Coast

My design client and friend Dee and my son Stephen fell in love with water-related living on separate paths of adventure in life.

Dee's story led her family from Chicago on the shore of Lake Michigan to Toronto to proprietorship of a hotel in the radiant Caribbean, and finally, to a land life in Marietta, Georgia. Her love of ocean living remains evident in her current home's design with a focus on natural aspects of nature.

Ocean Life Redefined

Dee and I designed this space and updated it over the years with nature-inspired art, accessories, soothing colors, and textures. The whimsical and modern art create a setting for worldly conversations and entertainment in the heart of Dee's home.

The living room furnishings in Dee's home are refreshing, sophisticated, and yet laid-back.
The silk plaid and floral fabrics are timeless.

The asymmetrical exclusive original art catches your eye as you enter the room.

The vibrant shade of coral brings the dining room center stage. Symmetry, texture, and Dee's favorite colors flow together in the room. The space is the perfect setting to share reflections with friends about experiences they are thankful for in life.

PART 2

A Coastal Sanctuary

Stephen and his family set up east coast roots on the Atlantic Ocean in the luxurious, historical district of Poppasquash in Bristol, Rhode Island. The area is known for its beautiful ocean views, boat building, marine industries, and tourism. Stephen attended law school at Roger Williams University, named after Rhode Island's founder, and decided from day one that this was the life for him.

Nature provides the contrast for lasting first impressions of Stephen's family's home in Poppasquash.

Contrasts are unexpected, and they create a kind of energy.[8]
—Designer Suzanne Kasler

Ocean views surround the home. Luxliving at its best!

The striking and sensational open living and dining room are design projects in progress that provide a perfect setting for relaxation. The luscious ocean blue upholstery Hickory Chair sofas were purchased through *The Furnished Room* in Roswell, Georgia.

Modern touches and mood lighting set the stage for a relaxing evening.

The roomy master bathroom is sheathed in white tile and paint.

Sensational windows continue to remind one of the setting while
soaking in the luxurious tub or relaxing in the shower.
Storage anyone? No need to clutter here!

Everyone's dream closet!

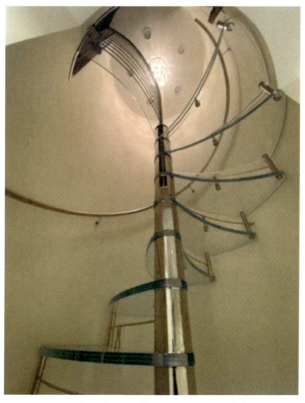

The inventive glass staircase provides the pathway to one of the massive closets in the home.

The view is worth a thousand words and a glass of wine.

Windows in a variety of shapes provide the feeling of outside living inside for friends and family.

Liz's cozy corner of the world is a great place for those of us who dream about relaxing by the ocean.
Picture of the ocean was purchased at *Vinings Gallery* in Roswell, Georgia.

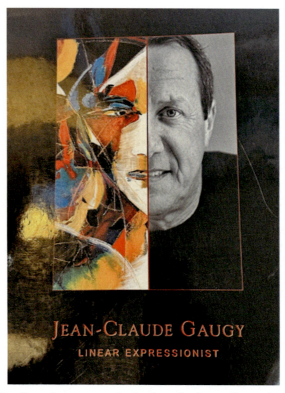

Lets face it: each of our homes exclusively tells the style and story of our lives.
Another fabulous picture purchased by Liz at *Vinings Gallery*!

ACKNOWLEDGMENTS

Great design touches lives. As a designer, I relate to the old adage, a house divided against itself cannot stand… When creating dazzling, sophisticated homes, personal visions need to be shared and taken to heart.

I am thankful for my parents who literally dropped-off me and my siblings at awe-inspiring museums, libraries, and ornate theatres as children.

I am forever grateful to my family, especially my partner in "design project crime" Gary Wenzel who lovingly strengthened my determination to complete the book.

I continue to be inspired by designers Jan Showers, Suzanne Kasler, Amanda Nesbit, Candice Olson, Barbara Westbrook, James Michael Howard, and Betty Lou Phillips.

An enormous thank you to my incredible clients and builders who became lifelong friends, especially those in the book - Elizabeth Basil, Jennifer Doxy, Bob Jamieson, Adam Jett, Dee Nolen, Stephen and Mira Patti, Elizabeth Pitcher-Hayob, Lauren and Scott Tompkins, Gail and Neal Cone, and builder Jennifer Blomquist. Special thanks to Lauren Tompkins who helped edit the book.

Thank you to all the vendors who made our dreams homes come to life including The Romo Group, Thibaut, F. Schumacher, Jim Thompson Showroom, Wallpaper and Stuff, The Curtain Exchange, Progressive Lighting, Westside Market, Sarah Cyrus Home, DK furnishings, Antiques and Beyond, Ballard Designs, Ben's Antiques & Market, Vinings Gallery, Classic Homes, Scotts Antique Market vendors, Floorworks Lighting, Jose Martinez and team, Jamie Whitehawk, and photographers Paul Zimmer and Brittany Dixon.

Thanks to the real estate agents and brokers who encouraged me to teach my courses on home design and supported my design passion, Debbie Nettles, Carolyn Fern, Dee Stamps- Auston, and Kelly Moran.

I appreciate Archway Publishing from Simon and Shuster experts who supported me throughout the book process especially concierge Deena Capron, the Editorial and Design staff, and Dennis Price, publishing consultant.

I feel blessed that Jenna Muller, Publisher of Modern Luxury, wrote the Foreword for the book.

In the end, Interior design is like a mystery to be solved by passionate people who love the good life. I encourage you to add dazzling design touches to your life.

BIBLIOGRAPHY

"Candice Olson Quotes." BrainyQuote.com. Accessed December 13, 2022. https://www.brainyquote.com/quotes/candice_olson_664352.

Fisher, Lauren Alexis. *Karl Lagerfeld's Wittiest, Most Iconic, and Most Outrageous Quotes of All Time*. California: Harper's Bazaar, 2020.

Kasler, Suzanne. *Inspired Interiors*. New York: Rizzoli, 2009.

Nesbit, Amanda. *Dazzling Design*. New York: Abrams, 2012.

"Oprah Winfrey Quotes." BrainyQuote.com. Accessed Date. https://www.brainyquote.com/quotes/oprah_winfrey_173381.

"Oscar de la Renta Quotes." BrainyQuote.com. Accessed December 11, 2022. https://www.brainyquote.com/quotes/oscar_de_la_renta_227349.

Phillips, Betty Lou. *Unmistakably French*. Layton, UT: Gibbs Smith, 2003.

Porter, Katherine Anne. *Ship of Fools*. Boston, MA: Little, Brown and Company, 1962.

Showers, Jan. *Glamorous Living*. New York: Abrams, 2020.

Walker, Alice. *In Search of Our Mothers' Gardens: Womanist Prose*. San Diego: Harcourt Brace Jovanovich, 1983.

Westbrook, Barbara. *Gracious Rooms*. New York: Rizzoli, 2015.

"Oscar de la Renta Quotes," BrainyQuote.com, accessed December 11, 2022, https://www.brainyquote.com/quotes/oscar_de_la_renta_227349.

Alice Walker, In Search of Our Mothers' Gardens: Womanist Prose (San Diego: Harcourt Brace Jovanovich, 1983),

Katherine Anne Porter, Ship of Fools (Boston, MA: Little, Brown and Company, 1962),

Jan Showers, Glamorous Living (New York: Abrams, 2020), page 94.

Barbara Westbrook, Gracious Rooms (New York: Rizzoli, 2015), 100.

"Candice Olson Quotes," BrainyQuote.com, accessed December 13, 2022, https://www.brainyquote.com/quotes/candice_olson_664352.

Amanda Nesbit, Dazzling Design (New York: Abrams, 2012), page 10.

Lauren Alexis Fisher, Karl Lagerfeld's Wittiest, Most Iconic, and Most Outrageous Quotes of All Time (California: Harper's Bazaar, 2020),

"Oprah Winfrey Quotes," BrainyQuote.com, accessed date, https://www.brainyquote.com/quotes/oprah_winfrey_173381.

Betty Lou Phillips, Unmistakably French (Layton, UT: Gibbs Smith, 2003), page 13.

Suzanne Kasler, Inspired Interiors (New York: Rizzoli, 2009), 52.
Kasler, page 72.

AUTHOR BIOGRAPHY

Imagine **Elaine Roberts** as a child dropped at the Toledo Museum of Art to spend her day amid classical art and vintage tableaux, followed by childhood memories of her grandmother's Old West End historical home. Encouraged by her parents toward two careers in higher education and in design, that lead to an Allied ASID and a Ph.D. in Literacy and Culture, prompting Elaine to create a three-hour credit course for the Georgia Real Estate Board entitled *Capitalizing on Home Design Tools for Faster Better Sales Results*. Author of several books, Elaine Roberts is a member of the American Society of Interior Designers and the creator of *Elaine Roberts Interiors*. Elaine was honored in 2020 as an ASID Industry Insider by the magazine *Modern Luxury Interiors Atlanta*. The *Elaine Roberts Interiors* booth at Scott's Antique Market in Atlanta was where Elaine was found each month sharing her inspirations with buyers, clients, and other vendors. She recently moved to San Antonio to live near her family and pursue new design endeavors.

Lauren Tompkins attended The State University of New York (SUNY) at Canton. She has experiences working in theatre, film, and in the financial sector. She enjoys reviewing texts and offering creative revision suggestions. Lauren is married to Scott Tompkins and has three wonderful children Dylan, Nathan, and Piper. She resides in Texas.